60p

# CONTENTS

Iwan Davies.

# THE TOPICAL TIMES

# FOOTBALL BOOK 1972-3

D. C. THOMSON & CO. LTD.
LONDON ● GLASGOW
MANCHESTER ● DUNDEE

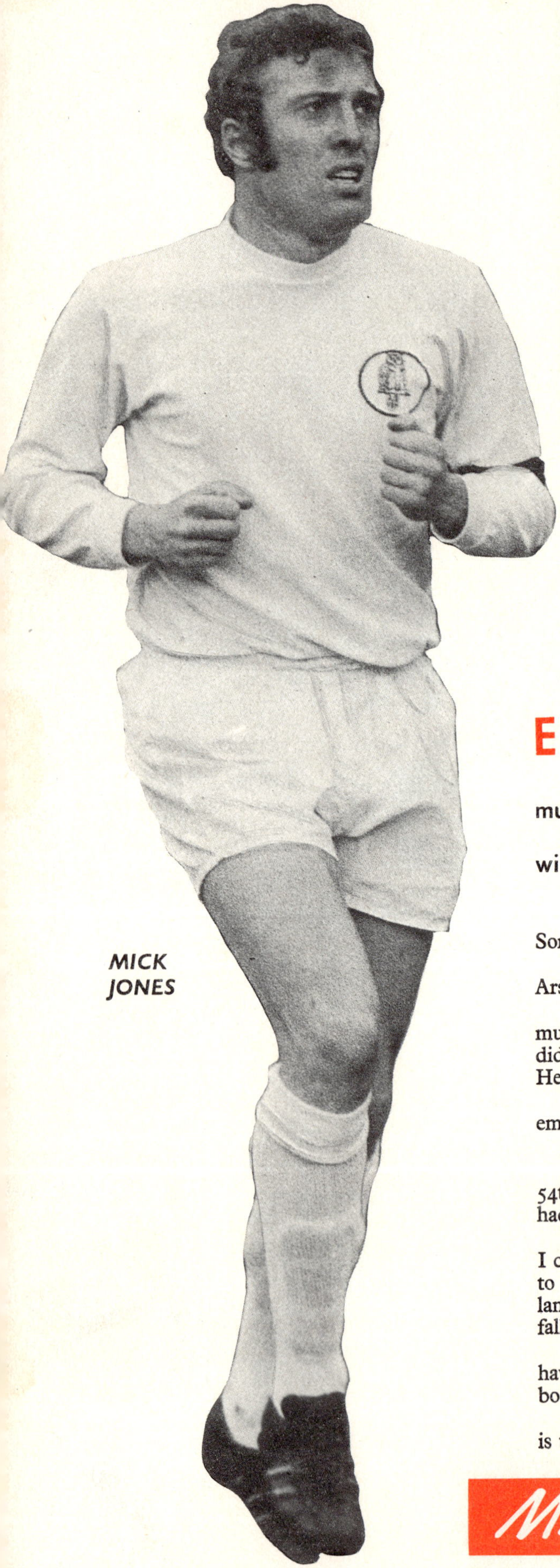

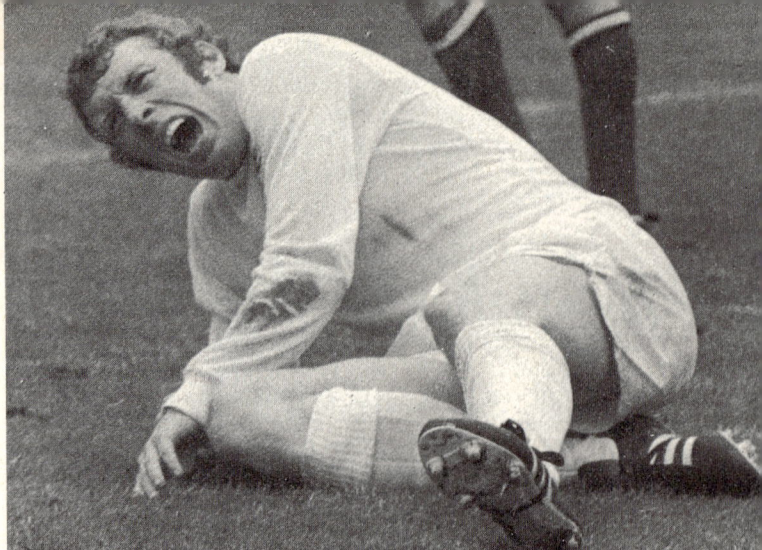

MICK JONES

*Immediately after the accident—"I never felt so much pain in my life. My elbow had been fractured."*

# WHEN THE

EVERY player must leave the game with an outstanding memory.

If he has played in a Wembley final, then that must surely be it.

Particularly if he has finished up on the winning side.

Like me . . .

But a Cup Final memory can come in all shapes and sizes. Some downright painful. Yes, even in triumph.

Which brings me to the 6th of last May. The day we beat Arsenal in the F.A. Cup Final.

I've got a winner's medal to show for it. But even today, so much of what happened remains pretty much a blur. Except that I did what I'm sure no other footballer in history has done—kept Her Majesty the Queen waiting!

Believe me, that's one Wembley reminder that still causes me embarrassment.

But let's go back to the beginning of this amazing episode . . .

There was barely a minute to go. We were leading 1-0. In the 54th minute I had crossed a ball from the right and Allan Clarke had sent a header thundering past Geoff Barnett in the Arsenal goal.

We had already got the signal the final whistle was near when I chased a ball into the Gunners' penalty area. Barnett came out—to reach the ball at the same time I did. I pitched over his body, landed awkwardly on my left arm—and felt the Wembley roof had fallen in on me.

I've had many falls like it and never even got a bruise. There have been many times when I thought I'd broken every bone in my body and got to my feet perfectly all right.

But my elbow was fractured—and the only thing I remember is that I've never had so much pain in my life.

*Mick Jones, Leeds United*

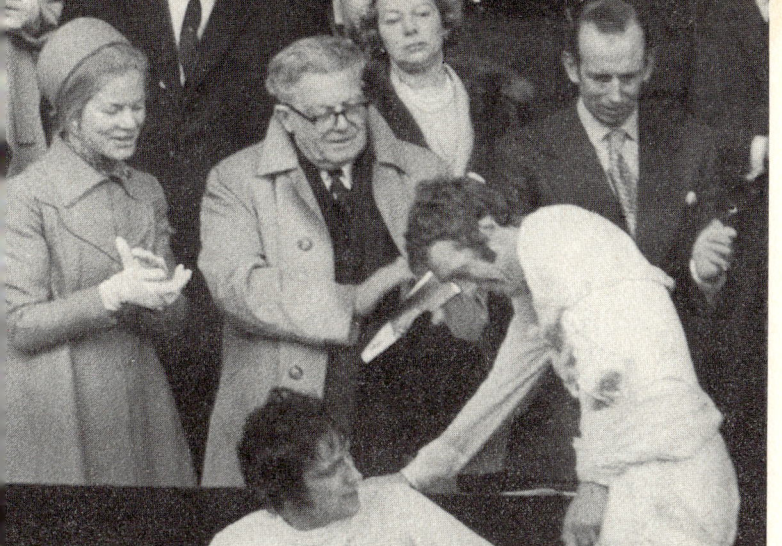

Leaving the Royal Box after meeting the Queen. "Hang on to my shoulder," says Norman Hunter.

# ROOF FELL IN AT WEMBLEY

A helping hand from the Leeds doctor —" Then I was whipped away on a stretcher."

I didn't even hear the final whistle blow. But a tremendous roar came through to me—and I remember thinking Arsenal had equalised.

Then there was a forest of legs around me. People were shouting and pushing. And Les Cocker, the Leeds trainer, was bending over strapping my arm to my side.

It wasn't until I was helped to the bottom of the steps to the Royal Box and saw the last of the Arsenal boys coming down with their medals that I realised we'd won the cup.

Then Mick Bates, our substitute, came up to me. " I've got your medal," he said.

I turned and told him I was going up there to the Royal Box.

I didn't realise I was keeping Her Majesty waiting or I'd have thought twice about going up. It was just the thought that the rest of the lads had been up for their medals and I hadn't even seen the Queen.

There was a great deal of swift debating about whether I could make it. But eventually Norman Hunter supplied the answer.

" Hang on to my shoulder," he said—and helped me up the steps.

I remember going up there, but I don't remember much about what was said—or about coming back down.

I know I was swaying about at the bottom of the steps and someone said, " Stand still, they're playing the National Anthem."

Then I was put on a stretcher and carried to the treatment room next to the Wembley dressing-room.

7

# THE "DOUBLE" BID I COULDN'T MISS

I was all right when being carried along, and managed a few waves to the crowd. I couldn't have done that if I'd been walking. My legs felt like jelly.

I was semi-conscious when they lifted me off the stretcher for an X-ray. Then I waited for what seemed like ages for the plate to be developed.

I heard all the lads singing next door, and wished the doctors would hurry up with that X-ray. I was beginning to feel really ill.

I never gave the cup a thought at that time. I only wanted them to put my arm back into place.

There was quite a lot of pain when that was done, but I got up and staggered into the packed dressing-room.

That was the first time I'd been on my feet since stumbling down the Royal steps. I was still groggy, showed it—and was helped across the room and told to lie down on the bench in the corner.

Eventually Les Cocker helped me into the bath and washed me down. By that time the rest of the team had finished and I had the tub to myself.

Les had to dry me afterwards as well, and had also to help me on with my clothes. I think I'd had something pumped into me. I felt very dopey.

With a vital league championship match against Wolves due on the Monday, the team was going to Wolverhampton from Wembley via our cup final head-quarters at Hendon. There they were to have a meal.

I went back with them in the coach as far as Hendon, picked up a few things, then returned to the London hotel where our wives and the Leeds officials were staying.

The game at Molineux, just 48 hours after our Wembley appearance, was an opportunity for Leeds to become only the third team in modern history to pull off the League and F.A. Cup double. But I knew I wouldn't be out there to help them in the second leg.

I went to bed when I got back to the London hotel and tried to watch the Cup Final recording on TV. I'd have given anything to have seen myself going up the steps so I could get an idea of what happened.

I travelled back to Leeds the next day. And even though I normally dislike watching the team play, I made a point of asking Mr Revie if it would be all right to travel down to Wolverhampton on Monday.

*Menace on the opposition goal-line. JACKIE CHARLTON takes up his corner-kick position. Arsenal players around him (left to right)—CHARLIE GEORGE, JOHN RADFORD, PAT RICE and BOB McNAB. Arsenal 'keeper, GEOFF BARNETT, is behind Charlton.*

# The Joy Of Cup Victory—

## —as demonstrated by ALLAN CLARKE

I was determined to be there to see if we could get the one point that would clinch the title—and therefore the double.

With that point we would have gone ahead of Derby County on goal average and would have remained ahead of Liverpool, irrespective of their result against Arsenal at Highbury.

I travelled down to the Midlands on Monday afternoon with club secretary Keith Archer, and watched the game from the stand, along with our full-back Terry Cooper. He, of course, was out of action with a broken leg.

I said I didn't like watching the team play. I know I'll never go to another Leeds game after seeing that one. It was torture.

We were beaten 2-1. And as Liverpool only managed a draw with Arsenal, Derby County became champions.

You can imagine our disappointment after coming so close to the double. We hadn't failed because we played badly. It was the circumstances that had piled up which caused us to miss out on the double.

## THE FANS WERE HAPPY

To begin with, the game shouldn't have been played so soon after our Wembley appearance. But the League insisted it be staged that night because of Wolves' U.E.F.A. Cup commitments.

We went out with around eight fit players. I was amazed how well the lads played after an hour and a half on the tiring Wembley pitch just two days before.

I think it's fair to say most of us would have preferred to win the league to the cup. Yes, even though the Wembley final has more glamour to it.

I would like to think we'll get as good a chance of winning the double again. I certainly believe that if the Wolves game had been two days later, on the Wednesday instead of the Monday, I would have had another championship medal to add to the one I got three years ago.

In the end, we all made up our minds it was only because the fixtures were so close together that we missed out.

But Leeds' supporters seemed very satisfied with the way things turned out.

I do believe the fans wanted us to bring home the cup more than they wanted the League trophy. Because the city had never seen the F.A. Cup.

I never even saw the trophy until the Monday after the final. But I hung on to that medal for a good while on the Saturday.

It will always remain one of my most treasured souvenirs.

# SKI-JUMP STYLE

## by PETER OSGOOD

**H**OW about this camera shot of the Chelsea centre-forward as he jumps to head a beauty at goal!

See how the posture compares with our ski-man in full flight.

**He's up to the knees in mud — but for BOBBY MOORE the end product is more big money . . .**

# FOOTBALL'S ONLY HALF THEIR BUSINESS

SOME people get themselves born at the right time — with the right talent to be a success.

It happened to George Best . . .

The magic in his feet made him a great footballer. The huge soccer boom following England's winning of the World Cup in 1966 came when he was just 20 and ripe for becoming a hero figure.

His particular looks, long hair and up-to-date clothes made him the trend-setter the young were looking for.

And the ever-alert George saw another side to it all—business.

First "toe-in-the-water" approach was the opening of a boutique. You heard the sonic bang of success in places far from Manchester.

The boutique is still there—in a modest, off-centre street in his adopted town. But now, instead of being the centrepiece, it's mostly of historical interest as the spot where "Besty" took off in the big-biz world.

Recently this, and additional boutiques, were absorbed by a clothing group . . . with no financial pain to George.

Among merchandise being sold is a suit costing £400. It's got thin stripes of 24 carat gold running through the material!

George keeps saying, "Men are becoming more interested in dress with every day that goes past." And the more interested they become the more his bankers, accountants and business associates will beam on the soccer marvel from Belfast who has become a tycoon in clothing, sports equipment, leisure wear, newspaper writing, advertising, film work—and television coaching for youngsters.

Not that it has all fallen in his lap.

Business associates will tell you he is no puppet to

★ Bobby is pictured here when early excavations were made for his country club project.

# A £2 SHIRT STARTED IT ALL . . .

be manipulated by the many sharp characters who hang around all personalities.

He knows the businesses he's in—and works at them.

It is estimated that, from a £1 million turnover on his businesses this year, George will get £50,000 or more. Add to this his Manchester United wages—certainly no less than £10,000—and you'll see why he had a £36,000 specially designed house in Bramhall, Cheshire, and drives about in exotic cars like a Jaguar V-12.

Summing up the situation, George says, " My job is to play football, but . . . in years to come it's business that will bring in the money."

Norman Hunter, Leeds United's most professional of professionals, has played close to 20 times for England.

On roughly three times that number of occasions he has been deputy to England skipper Bobby Moore.

Norman says of Bobby, " No one can exaggerate what this fellow has done for his country."

Equally, Bobby has made his contribution to soccer history pay-off.

Out of a £2 shirt has grown a Moore " empire," with an estimated income to Bobby of at least £20,000 a year. Some say double that.

The £2 shirt? Oh, that was Bobby's first " perk " for an advertising job. He posed in front of a house he had just bought. Pictures were taken for a publicity-conscious house agent. The agent gave him the shirt when it was all over.

Nine years later it is known Bobby has been paid £1500 for a day's work in a film studio advertising a hair tonic.

And he topped that when he later earned £9000 in fees one afternoon for sponsoring three other products.

Bobby's interests are wide.

He is in on television advertising, modelling, newspaper and magazine articles, an annual football book, a sports shop opposite West Ham's ground, a clothing business, a country club.

His company is Bobby Moore, Ltd. There are just two directors—Bobby and his partner-agent, Jack Turner. Jack is a life-long West Ham fan, and also got Bobby the £2 shirt on that first job.

Bobby lives in a £20,000, five-bedroomed house in Chigwell, Essex, with his wife, Tina, a model, and their family.

He says of his football-business life, " Football will occupy most of my life until I finish playing."

I don't know who'll be the first British soccer millionaire. But I WILL tell you this.

If anyone beats Manchester City and England hot-shot Francis Lee to it they'll be going some.

" Franny " didn't wait until he hit the big time before getting cracking on off-field interests.

At age 20, on modest wages from Bolton Wanderers, he started building up what is now one of the biggest wastepaper firms in Lancashire.

He is sole owner, which is fitting, seeing it was his

hard graft that built the business. It now employs a staff of 12, including five lorry drivers.

An objective man, Lee can compartment his life neatly between on-the-field and off-the-field calls.

Manchester City bought him for £60,000. This allowed him to break through to the big-time soccer he loves so much, but still stay in the Bolton area—nowadays in an elegant £20,000 thatched cottage in his home village of Westhoughton.

Franny will not discuss his earnings either on or off field. But, if you say between £10,000 and £15,000 for football, and a lot more than that from the waste-paper business, a boutique in Manchester, a ladies' hairdressing salon, advertising, films and newspaper articles, you'll be on the right lines.

At 17, Francis Lee could have had a drawing-board job. But he decided to go into senior football—because he fancied his chance more there of earning his target of £40,000 by age 34.

With six years to go, he's long past that !

In any list of top ten footballers of the 1960's must come the name of Dave Mackay, inspirer of double-winning Spurs and the Derby County he captained from low in the Second Division to high in the First.

In any list of top ten businessmen-footballers must also come the name of this hardy Scot who started his career with Hearts and sandwiched Spurs and Derby in between them and his present post as player-manager of Swindon Town.

While Dave insists, " My tie business is just a sideline," it is a fact this business, in London, grosses at least £60,000 a year from making ties, scarves, club badges—and employs a staff of 16.

Because of the Swindon job, estimated to be worth £16,000 a year, incidentally, Dave can only manage about 12 hours a week to the business these days. But in those 12 hours he goes through a power of work.

He also has an interest in a roofing contractor's business in Tottenham and property in Spain.

At 38 years of age, Dave's playing career is much, much nearer the end than the beginning . . . but should he have to leave the game tomorrow—though that is most unlikely—he'd have plenty to occupy his attention.

Working hard to get into the tycoon bracket is Manchester United's Willie Morgan.

He started with a laundrette . . . now has two. There's also part-ownership in a Manchester night club and interest in the modelling and designing of clothes.

Among others who have broken away from the play-for-ten-years-then-open-a-sweet-shop days of the limited wage for footballers are :

Alan Mullery, Don Rogers, Alan Kelly, Alan Spavin, Peter Bonetti, Peter Shilton—sports goods businesses ; Malcolm Allison, Colin Bell and Colin Waldron, restaurants ; Paul Madeley, wallpaper and paint business ; Alan Hinton, knitwear supplier ; Peter Dobing and John Ritchie, pottery business ; Pat Crerand and Denis Law, tyre agency ; and Mike Channon, ladies' hairdressers.

Changed days in the football world . . .

IMMACULATE WHITES—
for the Charity
Cricket Match.

DINNER-JACKETED—
for the special
evening occasion.

BLACK VELVET
SUIT—at an F.A.
disciplinary
session.

# BEST DRESSED
## —FOR THE OCCASION

ANYTHING GOES—
on holiday in
Majorca.

MOD GEAR— a demonstration
with two young friends.

CHEF'S RIG—
at a bakery
opening ceremony.

# OUT OF THE BLUE—

## COLIN BELL'S STORY

I felt like cheering.

I'm football mad — but even I have to admit the strain is tremendous nowadays.

A successful player with a successful club has a constant succession of big games with something at stake. What it boils down to is a break of, at most, four weeks in the summer. Four weeks in which to unwind and recharge for the next season.

It has to tell some time . . . as it told on my Manchester City and England team-mate Francis Lee, by the end of last season.

As I said, I captain City. That's a privilege, too. And made much more interesting when you have characters like Francis, Mike Summerbee and Rodney Marsh in the team.

They are brilliant players—and captaining brilliant players isn't hard. If things aren't going just right for us, one of them is sure to turn on a bit of magic. There's no need for a captain to tell them what is needed.

## MY SPECIAL CRITIC

Yes, I like being captain—though NOT the off-field side of it. My predecessor, Tony Book, was a great skipper on and off. He took the social side in his stride—attending functions of all sorts.

I'm different. Playing is my business. Outside it I have my business interest—my restaurant on the outskirts of Bury which I run along with Colin Waldron of Burnley.

One thing I wasn't too happy about was my form for the major part of last season.

I came back from the 1970 World Cup in Mexico fitter than ever I have been in my life. Then I " did " my cartilage, broke a bone in my foot, kept getting other niggling knocks.

One way and another, I had a poor season by the standards I set myself. I hope I can keep on wavelength this season.

If I don't, rest assured I'll hear about it from my sister, Eileen.

I**T was quite a day — that May day of last season.**

I had played for England against Wales. Over the next few days I noticed Sir Alf Ramsey looking at me a time or two, and thought—" You're going to be left out against Ireland, lad."

Instead, I was made captain of my country !

Now I have always been ambitious in football. I have always wanted to win things, to be captain of whatever club team I'm in.

But I never ever let myself contemplate the job of captaining England.

That was TOO big. It can only happen to the very, very occasional player. To reach the England team is such an honour in itself that thinking the one step higher doesn't come into it.

But I made it . . . and even though we lost to Ireland that night no one can ever take away from me now that I captained my country.

The way I got the captaincy was typical of Sir Alf Ramsey.

I was, as I say, thinking on the chances of being dropped. I knew Bobby Moore was unfit to play, but the thought farthest from my mind was that I'd replace him.

Then came a tug at my sleeve. It was Sir Alf. I was edged aside and asked, " How would you feel about taking over the captaincy?"

" Nothing I'd like better," I replied.

" Good, you've got it then," said our team boss.

# — SIR ALF MADE ME . . .

# CAPTAIN OF ENGLAND

When I was playing schools' football in the North-East my father didn't come along to see me in case he put me off. Eileen came instead, and became both a fan of mine and a critic.

She is married now, but there is no lessening of her interest. I'll phone twice a week as always. And, for sure, she'll have seen me play on television.

She'll take something I did . . . or more likely didn't do — and ask me why. Get me thinking about it. She very seldom gets it wrong, very seldom fails to help me improve on some aspect or other of my play.

She saw me a lot on television towards the end of last season, of course. In the West Germany games and the home international tournament. In many ways, these were my most important 'nationals.

I went into them with over a dozen England games behind me, but still not feeling I'd arrived as an England player.

I believe I did fairly well overall in the games. But, much more important from my personal viewpoint, I really felt at home at last.

It always takes me time to settle into a new environment. It happened when I joined City. It happened when I started with England.

But, whereas you can get used to things after a very few weeks with a club — because you are living that life constantly — it isn't so easy with England.

There are only so many internationals, so few chances to get deeply involved. But, possibly because so many came together this time, I felt really settled in with the 'national squad.

Actually, I don't suppose I'll ever be an easy mixer off the field, but I'm a lot better than I was. For this I have to thank working in my restaurant.

At first it was a terrible effort for me to go and talk to diners. I hated it. But, gradually, I forced myself to go over and have a word.

It became easier. Suddenly I found I wasn't bothered. And things are getting better every week.

Bang on target — in a full-power shot for goal

# DYNAMITE...

## ... in Arsenal jerseys

THREE hundred and fifty four lb. of dynamite in Highbury's red and white jerseys have been exploding around opposition penalty areas for just over three seasons now.

Ray Kennedy and John Radford. Both six-footers. Radford a near twelve-stoner. Kennedy a heavy-weight 13 st. 4 lb.

Both brimming over with courage. Powerful of shot. Soaring higher than all others when they go roaring into the box. Rated most dangerous "twin strikers" in the business.

Kennedy, at 21, worthy of the title "A second Geoff Hurst." Radford, an England cap in 1969 as an "old-fashioned" winger, now in the middle of the attack.

Both helped put Arsenal back on the map in European Fairs' Cup success and the winning of the League and F.A. Cup double.

Ray Kennedy, an England Under-23 internationalist last season, is likely to be a first-squad member by World Cup time in 1974. He's a man who has really proved the "great" wrong.

As a 15-year-old, he was signed for Port Vale by general manager Sir Stanley Matthews.

**JOHN RADFORD** — the overhead route to goal.

"Sir Stan came to our home at Seaton Delaval, near Whitley Bay, and asked me to come to Port Vale," Ray will tell you. "It was tremendous. I couldn't sign quickly enough."

Two years later, he was told by Sir Stan he was being released — because shortage of cash dictated a cut-down in young players.

"At the time I was shattered," says Ray Kennedy.

So kid Kennedy went home to Seaton Delaval — determined to show Sir Stan he was one who should never have been let go.

He took a job at a sweet factory, joined up with his former club, New Hartley, and scored fifty-six goals in one season.

Along came the Arsenal, offered him a chance to move to London — and everything's been wonderful since.

### DIET WAS CANCELLED

During Arsenal's League and Cup double season it was felt Ray was putting on too much weight. It was suggested he go on a diet. Cut out the starches and fats. Shed a few lb. Gain extra speed.

He lost 7 lb. and went seven matches without scoring a goal.

"Forget all about the diet," he was told. "Eat what you like."

Back on went the poundage — and back came the goals.

Perhaps because they are so much of a partnership on the field, Ray and John are buddies away from the game.

Radford best sums up the approach of the pair in talking about his attitude to the half-chance that comes in a crowded penalty area.

"You never see any danger," he says. "Most chances crop up in a split second. You have no time to think of consequences. In you go . . ."

That's the true philosophy of a goal-scorer.

RAY KENNEDY
Arsenal

LEEDS UNITED have won renown as a great all-round team. But discerning watchers pick out one man as the key component — JOHNNY GILES, or "The Little Master," as he is known to his team-mates.

So many Leeds attacks begin with the astute Irishman picking the ball up in midfield before slanting through the eye of a needle for the benefit of goal-grabbers like Allan Clarke, Mick Jones and Peter Lorimer.

Leeds boss Don Revie saw this creative talent in Giles when Johnny was a run-of-the-mill winger with Manchester United. It took only £25,000 to get him to Leeds. He has proved one of the greatest bargains of all time.

"PENALTY," scream Wolves fans—and look for JIM McCALLIOG. The Scotland international forward has become spot-king of Molineux. A cold-eyed killer from the spot.

Says Arsenal 'keeper Bob Wilson—"He doesn't blast them like Francis Lee. He simply picks a corner and tucks the ball away inside the post. The 'keeper gets no chance to read his mind."

That's all so typical of the McCalliog game. When the action is hot, Jim is the boy to put his foot on the brake, slow it all down and despatch the lethal ball to put a team-mate clear.

His mates label him "The Thinker." A man whose every move has purpose.

**RON DAVIES, Southampton**

ROY McFARLAND, Derby County

# TOP MEN *from*

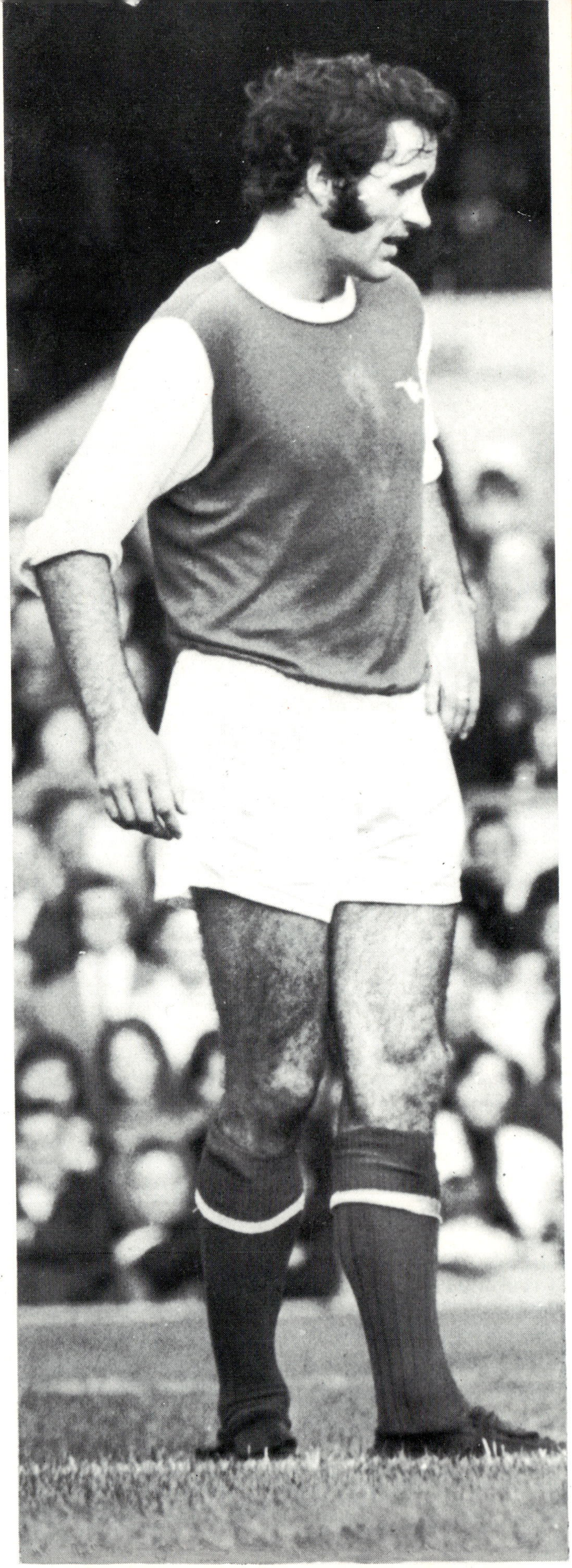

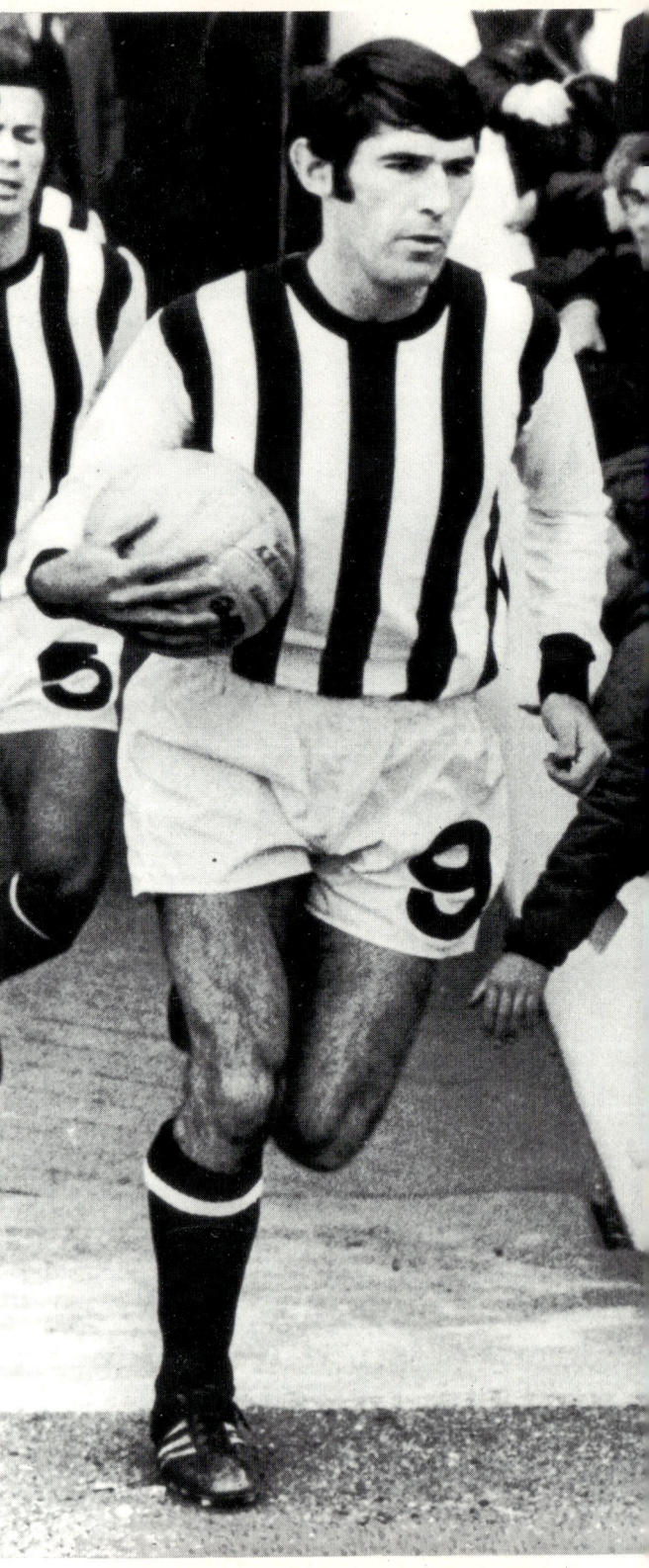

George Graham, Arsenal

Donald Ford, Hearts

# TOP TEAMS

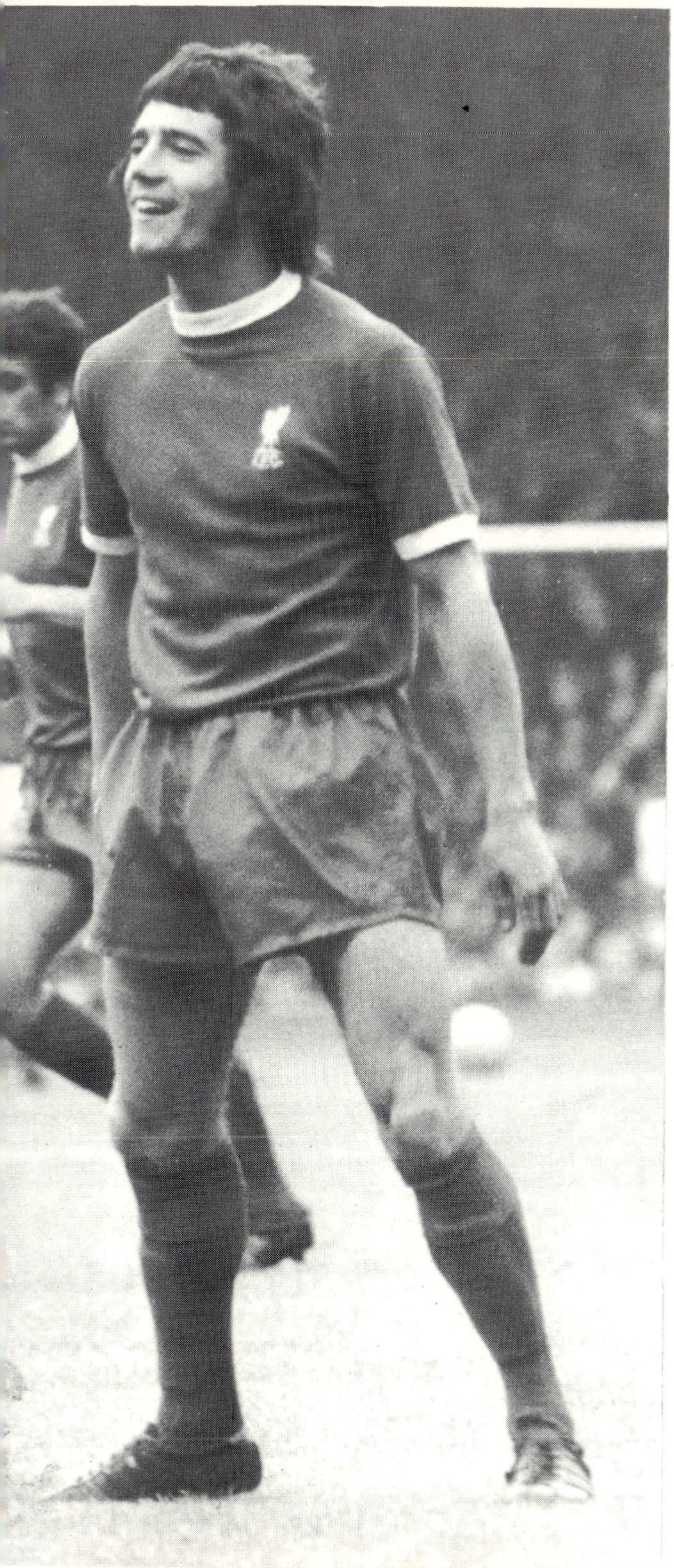

Kevin Keegan, Liverpool

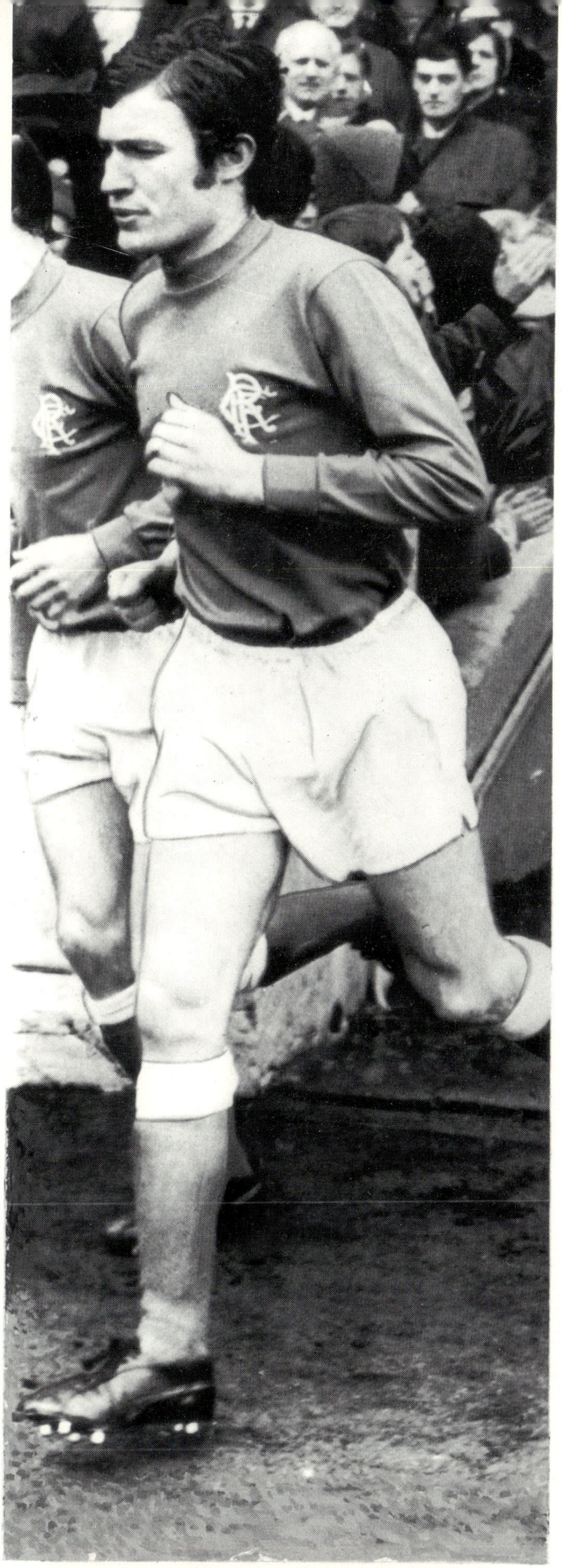

Sandy Jardine, Rangers

# The Camera Goes

**GEORGE BEST**
MANCHESTER UTD.

*A goal and it's aftermath*
( v SHEFFIELD UTD. )

**BOB WILSON**
ARSENAL

*—in a Royle occasion*
( v EVERTON )

# STAR·HUNTING

NAME KEY ON NEXT PAGE

**COKER in command — and
COKER in despair**

**S**ATURDAY, October 30, 1971 began like any other match day . . .

West Ham's team coach drew up outside Selhurst Park, the Crystal Palace ground.

The first-teamers — players like Bobby Moore, Geoff Hurst, "Pop" Robson, Clyde Best — strolled into the entrance hall.

It was just an ordinary league match for them.

I stayed with the coach. Helped unload the "skip" and pushed it in through the double doors and down the passage into the dressing-room.

Opening it up, I sorted through the shirts and shorts.

There were fourteen in the squad. The usual first-team line-up — minus injured 'keeper Bobby Ferguson — plus three youngsters along for the ride — Clive Charles (full-back), Dave Llewellyn (forward) and myself.

I had handed out eleven shirts and was wondering who was to wear 12 — when our manager, Mr Greenwood, came in.

He told everyone to sit down for a minute. Then he said . . .

"You may not know, but Geoff Hurst's back injury means he can't play today. We have to bring in a new face."

That was a surprise. I was reckoning Dave Llewellyn must take over, when Mr Greenwood turned to me . . .

"Get changed, Ade," he said. "We kick-off in 20 minutes !"

The shock was so great my legs seemed to turn jelly-like. I could hardly speak.

Geoff came over to give me back the No. 9 shirt I'd previously given him.

"Good luck, Ade, just play your normal game," he said.

The lads kept telling me not to worry.

Before leading us out, Bobby Moore came over.

"Don't worry about a thing," he advised me. "Just get a goal in the first couple of minutes and everything will be fine !"

---

**THE CAMERA GOES STAR-HUNTING**

Name key to pictures on preceding pages —
(1) GEORGE BEST — shooting a great goal despite the intervention of JOHN FLYNN (No. 4) — being congratulated by BOBBY CHARLTON (No. 9) — with ALAN GOWLING acclaiming the score — and JOHN ASTON (No. 11) and WILLIE MORGAN finally joining the party.
(2) FRANCIS LEE — overshadowed by MIKE CHANNON — getting in a shot though harassed by DENIS HOLLYWOOD, with MIKE SUMMERBEE looking on — standing guard over ERIC MARTIN — and turning away from HOLLYWOOD after an attack.
(3) BOB WILSON — on the ground, tangled with JOE ROYLE'S legs — a word in passing with ROYLE as JOHN ROBERTS arrives on the scene — same three, with ROYLE trying to block a throw-out — another admonition for the attentive centre-forward.

---

Next moment we were out on the pitch . . .

Around seven minutes had gone when Harry Redknapp took a corner. Palace centre-half John McCormick missed it. The ball hit defender Mel Blyth and dropped at my feet.

I'll never forget that moment. I hit it instinctively — and it went into the net like a bullet.

Man, a goal on your debut is like scoring the winner in the cup final. It was fantastic. What's more, the game was on television next day !

What more can a 17-year-old ask for ? A goal on his debut in front of the cameras. And a 3-0 win as well.

The goal settled my nerves. How I enjoyed that match — and my part in the tactical talk at half-time.

In the first half, I had been getting a lot of high balls to deal with. After the half-time talk, I started getting more at my feet to lay off.

● **"Get changed, Ade,"
ordered the manager.
"We kick off in
20 minutes."**

# ...and the
# hamper boy
# went out to
# hit a goal...

Things went well, with Billy Bonds and Clyde Best adding our other goals.

I was still in a bit of a daze after the game. It took the television replay next day to prove it was real!

It was really something to tell my brothers back home in Lagos, Nigeria. I'd come over to England with my parents and elder brother when I was 11 — leaving two brothers and a sister behind.

I looked forward to coming — but England was a big disappointment at first. Apart from the weather — which was cold — it seemed no different from back home.

It was a big upheaval at first. I wasn't too happy. But now I'm settled at West Ham it's all been ✦ worthwhile.

My ambition is to get a regular first-team place. At every opportunity I watch Geoff Hurst playing — trying to pick up tips. And I always study opposing players — like Peter Osgood, of Chelsea — hoping to learn something.

This is something that just isn't on in Nigeria. When I came over to England, I had hardly played any organised football. I've had to learn everything from scratch and catch up on boys who have been playing schools football much longer.

It's been hard, but I've been lucky to go to a fine club like West Ham. The club and the players have always been great to me. I've never felt conscious of my colour at Upton Park.

Perhaps having Clyde Best paving the way ahead of me has helped. We get along well together, because we've both had to work hard to adjust to English conditions.

West Ham reserve coach Ernie Gregory has helped us both a great deal — but we didn't always think so at the time.

Ernie is always having a "go" at us in training. At the time you feel he's never satisfied. That he'd still have a go even if you did everything perfectly.

Clyde is now established as one of the leading scorers in the country. My aim is to emulate him.

Looking ahead, I'm hopeful of playing international football — for Nigeria.

I'm told the Nigerian F.A. did approach West Ham after I made my debut — but they were told not to rush things.

The big problem would be getting to and from the matches if I were picked. But that's all in the future. I've got to win a place with West Ham first.

I'll certainly keep working on my game. Speed is my greatest asset at the moment. Now I'm working on turning with the ball and taking on opponents.

At the same time I've still to get used to winter conditions. In Nigeria all grounds are hard. If it rains it's usually enough to flood the pitch and stop the game altogether.

I'm always happiest at the start and end of the season. I still have difficulty playing in the mud. I find it difficult to judge the pace of a pass.

I know I've still got a lot to learn. Everything went right in my first League game. But I pretty soon learnt I was going to make plenty of mistakes.

And I hope I'm learning from them . . .

**Laugh-time for two big men of The Rangers — COLIN STEIN** *(left)*
**and JOHN GREIG**

# "An 80-game season is what I'd like," says Charlie Cooke of CHELSEA

## "We don't play enough football."

COOKE (with ball) and team-mate ALAN HUDSON.

I'M the last bloke in the world to disagree with experts.

But I'm not in line with some recent pronouncements in football.

Last season there was a crop of players who dropped out because of somewhat "mysterious" injuries.

Alan Ball (before he moved from Everton to Arsenal), Bob McNab (Arsenal), Mike Bailey and Hugh Curran (Wolves), Terry Venables (Q.P.R.), Alan Mullery (Spurs) and Francis Lee (Manchester City).

All big name players who had to call a halt because, it was said, of a too tough season.

Spurs even relegated Alan Mullery to the reserves. He felt so strongly about the situation he went to Fulham on loan, proved his fitness, was back in the Spurs side that won the U.E.F.A. Cup — and also won his place back to the England squad.

So much for pressures at the top.

Know what — before anyone in England had ever heard of Charlie Cooke, there was a bloke named Alan Gilzean playing for Dundee.

They sold him to Spurs at the end of 1964 — using some of the cash to buy a player named Charlie Cooke from Aberdeen.

At that time I did not know " Gillie." Last season he was a 34-year-old who was very much part of the

# Charlie's Charter

*In Chelsea's all-blue — and their change outfit of yellow*

Spurs' triumph in the U.E.F.A. Cup. Still turning it on at the end of a tough season — and no worries about playing too much football.

So much for the strain at the top.

I went to England nearly two years after Gillie — and I hope I can still be playing at the top at his age.

Gillie moved to the Spurs for £72,500. Dundee spent around £40,000 on me. And then I moved to Chelsea for about £75,000.

I hope I can justify it all by keeping going as long as Alan Gilzean.

## SQUADS TOO BIG

In spite of what the experts say, I don't think the average player plays enough matches a season.

British professionals think that they are over-worked if they clock up between fifty and sixty games over around nine months.

Players like Pele (Brazil) regard at least sixty matches a season as routine.

I met Pele when I was in Mexico for the last World Cup. We talked, and Pele made the point that you must pace your season.

He felt that by playing a lot of matches he did not need to get involved in too many training sessions. He kept fit by playing matches.

"It's a lot easier, too," he added.

I refuse to accept that British professional players are overworked. I feel we are underplayed — especially with a squad of eighteen first team players.

This is too big a squad for current needs. A longer season, with more matches, would mean all the squad being used.

I'd like to see a forty week season. With matches on Saturday, Wednesday (or whatever mid-week day suits) and Saturday. This is the kind of situation in which full use could be made of an eighteen-man first-team squad.

When matches are played at the week-end, you can get a knock on the Saturday and be ready for the next game. This would not happen were mid-week matches a regular feature. The entire squad could be used.

It would mean more money for the club — and a chance of more money for the players.

I don't think any professional would find eighty matches a season too difficult. But it would have to be a definite season. Forty weeks and then a two-month break.

I find the worst thing about the current set-up is that a player never knows when the season starts and finishes.

There is also the question of success.

When Arsenal won the League and Cup double they used very few players. Last season Leeds United were going for very much the same target. This means a lot of matches. But, when there's a winning sequence on, I'm sure few players want a rest. There is nothing like a winning team to " find " fit players.

This is where we come back to Alan Gilzean.

The Spurs were very much involved last season. Always in League contention, going a long way in the League and F.A. Cups, going all the way in the

# "THE DOC'S

U.E.F.A. Cup — plus a couple of additional start-of-season matches against Torino in the Anglo-Italian tournament.

Alan Gilzean missed very few matches — which is the kind of situation that keeps a 34-year-old very young.

It was much the same with myself last close season.

I thought I'd blotted my Scotland copybook when Scotland lost to Belgium in the 1969-70 season. I reckoned I would never again be included in a Scottish party.

Then along came Tommy Docherty — and I was invited to go to Brazil. Suddenly I felt the need for international football again.

I was back in the swim, and it's a great feeling. Even though I had to miss this Brazil trip through injury.

I'm not the kind of character who puts himself out on a limb by saying that I now feel Scotland

*'stached Charlie Cooke looms large in this action strip from big games of last season.*

will do very well. That way you get things thrown back in your face.

But I think Tommy Docherty will give Scotland a lift in international football. He'll certainly get the players chasing.

He was doing the same job when I first arrived at Chelsea. Then he had a " player " approach. Now I think he is a very much more mature character. I back Scotland as doing every bit as well as England when it comes to the World Cup in 1974.

But I won't stick my neck out.

I will say the team Scotland sends out will be playing as hard as any in the world. That should be at least enough to get us to the final qualifiers stage.

I don't want to harp on age, but this is something folk are apt to remind you of when you are an experienced player.

When I was playing in Scotland I seemed to run

# NJECTION

into a fair amount of trouble — mainly because I was apt to flare up and retaliate.

A newspaperman went along to my father and asked him what advice he would give the young Charlie Cooke.

" Keep the heid," he said.

I've always tried to do this ever since — translating the advice since I moved South to " Keep your head."

Now let's talk about Chelsea.

The very name brings to mind the swinging King's Road. The legend of Chelsea goes back to Scottish players like Hughie Gallacher and Alex Jackson. But it's an image that has been lost.

Our record in recent seasons hasn't been at all bad. For a start, there were our successes in the F.A. Cup and Cup-Winners' Cup.

Last season we seemed to be set for everything. Then, in the space of just over a week, we went out of

the F.A. Cup in the fifth round and lost to Stoke City in the final of the League Cup.

That's just one of those football happenings. It had nothing to do with Chelsea and the King's Road and all that goes on around there.

We seem to take a bit of time to get started in the season.

Tommy Docherty tried to sort out this trend when he was at Stamford Bridge. Dave Sexton has taken things a stage further. He allows no one to rest — stressing the most important award for Chelsea is the Championship. Any other honours are extras.

## A CIGAR IS HELPFUL

I'm now creeping up to 30 — and I have always had to live with something of a weight problem. I have a diet that means cutting down on liquid intake. And sometimes I smoke a cigar to cut down the urge to eat. That's not hard to take.

Jockey Lester Piggott, another weight-watcher, also goes in for a cigar when he feels need for a meal.

If someone asked me the biggest change I have found since moving to England, I'd rate it the new attitude by referees.

The rules that cut out tackling from the back and give players with skills a chance to work with the ball.

I've always been a ball player. As a youngster I was impressed with a man called Puskas. I used to read what he could do with a ball — and he was alleged to be a one-footed player.

I felt I had TWO good feet and should be able to do the same.

In Scotland we used to play a game called " keepie-uppie." I'd try to keep-it-up with both feet — reckoning that might help me into the top class.

I feel I have settled down over the past couple of seasons. I still like to hear the crowd start to murmur when I have possession. Still like to feel I can take on, and beat, a defender. Still feel that I cannot get enough football.

Perhaps that's the reason I differ from the medical experts.

32      **TREVOR HOCKEY,** Sheffield United

# THE TRANSFORMATION OF TREVOR

**W**E were sitting in this hotel waiting for a meal . . . and getting hungrier and hungrier.

When the waitress came through to apologise and say "It won't be very long now," one of my Birmingham City team-mates pointed at me . . .

"It had better not be," he said. "You never know what this fellow will eat if he gets TOO hungry."

Next time that waitress came through she got some shock . . . because I was sitting munching away at a daffodil from a vase on the table.

That was anything-for-a-giggle-and-a-bit-of-publicity Hockey. Now I'm more mature, though still very conscious of the need to "sell" football — for players to keep in touch with the fans.

Actually, the daffodil story rebounded on me a bit.

As soon as the waitress left the dining-room I spat it out. It tasted horrible.

But one of my team-mates was writing a column in a Birmingham paper and he mentioned the incident.

That did it.

From my fans all over the Midlands, the daffodils poured in!

I wrote to my fan club . . . yes, I had one of them as well . . . and said I'd say it with daffs, by return, on the Saturday.

## I WAS ONE OF THE ALSO-RANS

I was really in deep then. A player with a reputation for being anything but a softie running out with a bunch of daffodils in his hand before a game! I ask you!

Still, in these days it was in for a penny . . .

So out I went — my wee bunch of flowers tucked discreetly into the top of my shorts.

After a very, very short kick-about, I edged towards where my fan club stood and, as soon as I was within range, threw the flowers to them.

It went down a treat, without anyone taking the mickey.

I embarked on my publicity thing with Birmingham City — and quite deliberately.

I'd played with Nottingham Forest and Newcastle United. Had a big part in helping Newcastle win promotion to the First Division.

But both places I'd been just another player. Very much one of the also-rans when it came to the name-in-the-paper business.

So, when the move to Birmingham came about, I set my sights, quite deliberately, on being noticed.

1963—Nottingham Forest

1965—Newcastle United

1968—Birmingham City

c

# MY CAR CAUSED A SENSATION

I grew long hair for starters.

Not too way-out this, because it was the growing—excuse the pun—habit at the time.

But . . . who else had a pink piano with all the keys painted a different colour? Who else had a velvet-covered car? Who else sang in a pop group? Who else (ugh!) ate daffodils?

I wonder who has the piano now?

I had to leave it behind when we moved to Sheffield. So, if it has landed in your house, let me explain the different-coloured keys.

I had them that way to try learn music by colours!

You know . . . a certain colour a certain note.

It didn't work, but I still think it wasn't a bad idea.

The car I had covered as an advertising stunt.

It was sort of velvet. You brushed the surface clean instead of washing it!

What a sensation it caused.

When my wife and I went shopping, I'd sit in the car—intent on avoiding becoming involved with crowds. Fat chance . . .

That car was like a magnet. They'd spot it — and edge over. Then they'd touch the surface and the "ooh's" and "aah's" would start.

## THE ALL-COLOUR ROUTE TO PIANO-PLAYING

Next they'd look inside, see me and, before you could cough, there was a crowd bigger than we'd have got inside a shop.

You might think all this a bit irresponsible.

Don't believe it.

I was, if you like, the comedian of the team. In the sense that I'd do anything for a laugh, a bit of fun.

You see, I had complete confidence in myself. Always have had, and I hope always will have.

That isn't cockiness. Oh, no . . . that's a very different kettle of fish.

But I knew, at the height of my publicity spell with Birmingham, that I was doing well out on the field and that no one would object as long as I kept doing it there.

Now, I'm with the Blades . . . Sheffield United. Back home in my native Yorkshire—even though I've been capped for Wales lately because of my father being born there.

And I love it.

United are a great team—and international football has always been a desire of mine.

I don't do all that I did with Birmingham City any more. I mean, for instance, my car is a sort of average bright orange now!

I'm matured, I suppose.

Well . . . there is the hair-band, of course. Oh, I hadn't mentioned it? Well, it really only started last season.

At the start of training for the season it was very hot. I found my long hair getting in my eyes. Straggling down over my face. Annoying me.

I could, you'll say, always have got it cut off.

Maybe, but it's a sort of thing with me. I like long hair. I like my beard.

So, I wore an elastic band in training to keep the top hair out of my eyes.

It worked.

Came the start of the season and I thought—"That was O K in training, but I won't half get stick from the lads if I do it for a real game."

So, before the first game, I got into a corner of the dressing-room and slipped on a more sophisticated "hair-holder-downer" than a common rubber band—and turned to face the cat-calls.

They never came. No one seemed to notice. So I've worn my "band" ever since.

Crowds notice me, though. Away crowds particularly.

Though I don't pay much attention, I can't help being aware of some of the slightly (!!) uncomplimentary things they say.

I have what I call the Nobby Stiles philosophy to this.

Nobby used to say, the harder they boo me, the better I must be playing. So, long may they boo.

I enlarge a bit to say they're booing me . . . but it's in direct ratio to how loudly they'd be cheering me were I on their side.

When I came here, I went into the supporters' club. Above the bar there is a list of names. "What's that for?" I asked.

"These are the names of United players who have represented their countries," came the reply.

"I see there is one space left," I answered. "Keep it for me. I'll be getting a cap or two here."

And I did. For Wales — my father's native country. Tremendous. There is something special about being an internationalist.

Yet, in the same season, I come down with my leg-break — in February in a game against Manchester City.

I'm not moaning about that. When you do the job I do on the field — winning the ball for your team — you can't expect to get away without injury.

But a broken leg takes so long. I like my football so much. Being away from it even for a week or two is murder.

In fact, I lost three months. I never get depressed, but I was champing at the bit all the time.

I tried to make it for the home international tournament, but failed . . . by only two weeks.

Still, though I missed playing against England, we have another crack at them this season — in the World Cup qualifying games.

Munich '74. Now that would be just fine.

# GB..
## GORDON BANKS

# BG..
## BRITAIN'S GREATEST

**T**HEY used to say you had only to be daft to be a goalkeeper.

To spend ninety minutes on a bleak January afternoon shivering under the crossbar.

To throw yourself down among flashing studs — risking serious injury.

To be called a mug for one mistake on a day when you had pulled out half a dozen great stops.

But Gordon Banks of England, voted best goalkeeper in Britain, keeps on proving this specialist position demands as much skill, dedication and courage as any of the more glamorous football jobs.

His ability has made him a legend in the game. At 33, his dedication to training is a model for any young man starting out on a professional career.

# SAVE THAT MADE THE WORLD RAVE

Football fans around the world know the familar figure in the yellow jersey—prowling around the England penalty box. Few know the Gordon Banks who earns his bread and butter with Stoke City.

There are really two Gordon Banks. The one who can laugh and joke on the team bus to Wembley. And the unsmiling character who steps on field to build up total concentration for the game ahead.

His preparation in the dressing-room is always thorough and precise. His kit has to be perfect. A jersey that is loose to give freedom. Studs checked to match underfoot conditions. Gloves specially designed by himself to give sure grip on the modern plastic ball.

And always he has a ten-minute warm-up of stretch and bend exercises to make sure he never gets caught cold in the vital opening minutes.

During the game his concentration is so intense he can recall in detail moves and incidents that happened in matches months previously. Never does he relax—even though the ball is in the other half of the field.

Mentally he plays every move so he will never be caught napping by a quick break. If he feels concentration slipping during a long spell without a touch, he will slap and pinch his thighs and talk himself into full focus on the ball.

Boss of his area, he believes a 'keeper doesn't have to be an Aunt Sally waiting for opponents to fire in shots. He sets out to pressure attackers into shooting to where he wants the ball.

An opponent clean through will find Gordon kidding to go left—then reacting immediately the ball is sent to the right.

Although England's first choice for nine seasons now, he still works on the practice makes perfect principle—and has been known to turn up at the ground on Sunday mornings for extra work with the apprentices.

There have been so many great Banks' saves it is difficult to single one out as the greatest. But the TV cameras sent pictures of his wonder save from Pele in the 1970 World Cup round the globe. It has become part of football history.

The great Brazilian met a cross six yards out to power a header down into that killer spot for the 'keeper. A yard short of the line. Designed to leap up into the corner.

## SO REASSURING

Banks exploded down and across his line to flip the ball out and up—with the crowd behind the goal already rising to acclaim a score.

"The greatest save I have ever seen," says his England team-mate, Colin Bell. "In that moment we grew ten feet tall, knowing the Brazilians would be wondering what they had to do to beat this man."

Television caught another moment of Banks' greatness at West Ham last season when he saved a last-minute penalty from Geoff Hurst to give Stoke the chance of a successful third game on their way to winning the League Cup.

But it is not just the spectacular saves that make Banks great. It is his confident, precise work in all the little testing moments that can spell danger.

The nasty swinging cross picked out of the air so surely. The explosive shot taken straight into the chest —because he was in the right place. All so reassuring for the men in front.

Away from the game Gordon is a changed character. He can even pull out a brilliant imitation of comedy magician Tommy Cooper.

Always at the centre of things when jokes are flying on an England occasion, he once gave the Russian international team something to think about during a trip abroad.

Team boss, Sir Alf Ramsey, had come out on to the terrace of the hotel to give his players spending money for the day.

Suddenly Gordon jumped up and marched forward —army pay parade style.

*Banks at work — with a classic diving save. See how he gets hands perfectly behind the ball.*

# TAKING THE MIKE

Giving a name, rank and number, he came to attention and saluted the astonished Ramsey. But, taking his cue, the England boss returned the salute and handed over the cash.

As the Russian team watched open-mouthed at their windows, the entire England squad followed on to salute the manager before getting their pay. Goodness knows what the Russians thought of English discipline.

On long coach trips Gordon has been known to take the microphone and deliver a hilarious tourist guide sort of chat.

Once it was, " I do not wish to alarm you, gentlemen, but the smoke you see behind that hill to your left is made by an Indian war party."

Until recently Gordon never mixed business with football. Now he's accepting some offers in advertising and the like.

A family man, he lives in a splendid house in the quiet of the Staffordshire hills. Relaxation he gets in gardening or golf. He takes his golf seriously, too. A miscue with the clubs is sure to turn off the famous Banks grin.

## TOGETHER AGAIN

Having been around the international scene for so long, Gordon has friends throughout the country. And how he enjoyed landing up at the same club as his great mate, George Eastham.

The pair first got together as mates in the England squad when Gordon was with Leicester City and George with Arsenal. Stoke City manager, Tony Waddington, renewed that partnership by signing both.

Now the back-chat between the two is one of the features of the Stoke dressing-room. They even partner each other on golf outings—taking on all comers.

Any professional who has played with Gordon Banks will tell you his secret is hard work. At thirty-three he is training harder than ever to maintain strength and agility.

For instance, he always demands match conditions be applied to his training. He asks for crosses with a man to challenge him. Followed by every possible shot —from close-range blasters to chipped lobs. He will never knock a ball away casually. Always he goes flat-out to make the save and hold on if possible.

He works on simple things like goal kicking. Aiming to drop the ball on a two-penny piece, or throw it with the right curve to put the ball precisely into a colleague's path.

He insists on ten balls for his special 45-minute work-outs—each cleaned, polished, with weight and air pressure made exact.

He is also an enthusiast for five-a-side games. Liking nothing better than to get a chance to play outfield. And, as you'd imagine, he can hit 'em.

Some player, Gordon Banks . . .

**A Moment To Relax**

Awaiting events during an injury break, BOBBY MOORE, West Ham, looks completely switched off.

## COLIN TODD

# SUDDENLY, THE SILENT MAN REBELLED

*Manager BRIAN CLOUGH*

**Y**OU'D go a long way to find a quieter bloke than Colin Todd, gifted defender of England's top champions, Derby County.

This tough, fast, compact sweeper can only be called "The silent star of English football."

Indeed, his volatile boss, Brian Clough, says of him—"He just never talks — except when absolutely necessary. Never loses his temper. Never gets excited. Never crosses me — or his team-mates."

Clough shook the football world by paying Sunderland £170,000

International aces of the Baseball Ground — (left) — TERRY HENNESSEY (Wales), ARCHIE GEMMILL (Scotland) — (below) — ROY McFARLAND (England).

for Colin—a record fee for a defender. Even after six months at the Baseball Ground, the Derby boss was still perplexed by the silence of this Geordie . . .

" I swear I do not know what goes on inside his head.

" I have occasionally talked to him quite critically about his play. He just listens—then goes out and plays better than the last time."

It is this reluctance to speak at any length about the game and its problems that has kept Todd out of the headlines.

Colin's father died when he was a boy. He has striven hard to look after his mother.

An immediate hit when he strolled into the Sunderland first team at the age of 17, he quickly became an idol on Wearside.

" I started football as an inside-forward with my school at Washington, in County Durham.

Alan Brown was manager of Sunderland when I signed for them.

" At 15 years of age I remember Mr Brown coming with us for a youth tournament in Holland. He took a great interest in me, but I could see he was a tough disci-plinarian. I didn't mind that. But never did I realise that, in five years' time, I would be fighting Alan Brown to get away from Sunderland."

It was a bitter confrontation, too. Sunderland didn't want to lose a player of Todd's outstanding class.

He was never dropped from Sunderland's first team. He won 11 Under-23 caps while at Roker Park—then became the youngest club captain in the First Division. And Sir Alf Ramsey made him skipper of the Under-23 side.

But, as Sunderland slumped to

# A £170,000 DEAL—AT THE DOUBLE

**ALAN HINTON
— the Derby
winger with
the explosive
shot.**

the bottom of the First Division, Todd increasingly felt the pressure. So much was expected of him.

First he swept up behind 31-year-old Charlie Hurley, who was beginning to slow down. Then he had the totally inexperienced 17-year-old Richie Pitt alongside him. It was not easy.

On top of this there was his responsibilities as captain.

"Several times I asked to be rid of the captaincy. I simply didn't feel I had it in me to become a driving captain. That has never been my nature. But Alan Brown kept assuring me I had hidden qualities as a leader."

Then Sunderland were relegated. It was a blow to Wearside, and a shattering setback to Todd.

He did not want to play in the Second Division. Felt it would ruin his chances of winning a full England cap.

He wrote out a transfer request. It was turned down. He wrote another. Again it was rejected.

The quiet lad had turned quite tough . . .

"I know some people accused me of being disloyal to the club that had brought me into the game. I simply decided Sunderland in the Second Division was not good enough. *And I kept putting in transfer requests.*

"I was single-minded about these moves. It was not something I liked doing. But it had to be done."

Eventually Sunderland relented. On the day it was announced Todd was for sale, the quicksilver Brian Clough motored up to Sunderland and went straight to Alan Brown's house.

Colin takes up the story . . .

"At 7.30 in the evening, Mr Brown phoned to say he had a surprise for me. Would I come round to his house.

"I drove round. Brian Clough asked—would I sign for Derby. By 9 p.m. I was at the Sunderland secretary's home and had done the deed."

The cost to Derby was £170,000. That raised a few eyebrows, be-

cause that sort of money always went on forwards.

Peter Taylor, Derby assistant manager, said later—" We are sick of people ridiculing us for paying that record fee for Todd. Nobody ever thought we spent £30,000 of it purely on his character. We have a player who will give us 100 per cent. for the next eight years."

And at Derby Todd was to have his eyes opened.

He says, "First, there is the variety of training. Something totally different every day.

"But Friday in Derby always follows the same routine.

"We report to the ground at 1.45 p.m. Do one hour's training. Then straight from ground to a hotel — with dinner at 6.30 p.m. Bedtime is at 10.

"That never changes. It is an ideal build-up for a game. It keeps our minds on what lies ahead—without any distractions.

"Punctuality is another vital factor at Derby. Lateness for training—or anything else laid on by the boss—brings a fine. There are no let-offs."

At international level Colin Todd has been just as consistent as at club level.

Of the England manager, Sir Alf Ramsey, he says, "Although he made me captain of the Under-23 team, I hardly feel I know him. In fact, I was a little shy of him for the first five games or so. I used to go away and hide from him. But gradually I have got to know him better.

"Tactical talks by the three main managers in my career reveal so much about their personalities.

"Alan Brown would spend a lot of time telling us practically everything about the team we were going to play. He would go through the individual strengths and weaknesses from goalkeeper to outside-left.

"Sir Alf Ramsey will talk for a long time about tactics. Formations and the build-up to attacking movements—9 times out of 10 he outmanoeuvres the opposition.

"Our Derby boss, Brian Clough, tells us what we are going to do. He rarely talks about the opposition team or individual players. It's the US — US — US. What WE are going to do!"

# MINI-STRIKER

## - WITH A MAXI-PUNCH

This is LOU MACARI. Right—
fellow-striker KEN DALGLISH

Can you imagine wee Alan Rudkin taking on Muhammad Ali?

Impossible, you say.

Well, what Alan would be up against in a match like that is something like what I have to contend with EVERY WEEK!

Only, boxing isn't my game. It's football. To be exact—straight-through-the-middle striking.

And, often as not, the stern battle for goals—with three or four big defenders trying to stop you—can make that penalty area rough as any boxing ring!

Me, I'm 5 ft. 5 in. and weigh in at around 10 st. Which means that, every week, I'm up against opponents up to NINE INCHES TALLER and FOUR STONES HEAVIER.

So, is it any wonder that, when you're a wee yin

*" I've just got to be a hard-hearted hustler," says . . .*

## LOU MACARI - CELTIC

# WHEN THE "OLD PALS ACT" ENDS

like me, you've GOT to learn to look after yourself?

Of course, I wasn't always five-foot-five. As a schoolboy, playing for Scotland, I was just five feet! But even in those days I was aware I would have to do something special to make up for my lack of inches and pounds.

So I determined that whenever I challenged for the ball it was MINE. No question of the other fella winning it.

At school I wasn't a striker. I was an inside forward —fetch-and-carry style. That meant an awful lot of work on the park. Just like Billy Bremner and Archie Gemmill.

And, like Billy and Archie—as you can guess, I'm a great admirer of that pair—I've developed to the stage where I'm afraid of nobody.

That's not being boastful, just a statement of fact. I can't afford to fear an opponent. Football is my livelihood. It puts my breakfast on the table, pays my rent.

If I were to go on to the park with anything less than 100 per cent. conviction in my ability to come out tops, I would be as well to chuck it.

It's an attitude that has stood me in good stead over the years—though it CAN have its drawbacks.

For instance, I probably have more fouls awarded against me during a game than any other Celtic player. For the simple reason I COMMIT more fouls than anybody else.

You see, when I'm challenging inside the area, my elbows, hips and shoulders are all going. It's got to be that way, otherwise these big blokes would just brush me aside.

But I must say this—I probably get away with more fouls than I'm pulled up for.

That's one of the advantages of being small. Referees can't see everything that goes on at close quarters, especially when I'm three-quarters hidden by the big men I'm pushing!

Take that goal I scored for Scotland in the under-23 match against Wales at Pittodrie last season.

The ball came over from the right. I was in the middle of an army of defenders—practically standing on the goal-line.

I went up to try to back-head it into the net, saw I wasn't going to make it, shot out a fist—and PUNCHED it home!

The ref. gave a goal.

Because I get away with so much I rarely complain when decisions go against me. Referees are only human, they can't see everything.

And another thing—I would never try to hurt anybody. My hustling, jostling tactics might impede somebody, but they'll never break a leg.

That's one of the reasons I've rarely been in trouble. There's nothing malicious about the way I play. But, naturally, I get my share of abuse and insults on the field.

It's not the first time I've been chased by a big defender, determined to wring my neck!

And I remember a couple of years back being threatened with all sorts of physical damage by the TRAINER of a well-known First Division club!

It was a reserve match, and the big centre-half and I had been having a rare old tussle. A high cross came over and up we both went for it.

My elbows were sticking out like handlebars on a bike. One landed in the pit of the centre half's stomach. I didn't really mean that, but he was a bit winded and went down.

On came the trainer to give treatment. I came up to see how the big fellow was, and the trainer said, " I wish I was playing against you, you little ———. I'd break your scrawny neck!"

Of course, my height—or lack of it—can produce its funny moments. Take the friendly we had with Nacional of Uruguay last year. They were then world club champions.

Well, every one of their players was a big, athletic ball player. I'll never forget the look of shock on the big sweeper's face the first time I challenged him for the ball!

Because I nearly knocked him flat on his back.

Then there are the times I go racing. That's my only other great passion. I don't drink, don't smoke, don't go out socially very much. Racing is my one luxury. I go whenever I can.

I'm glad I'm not a jockey. Because I feel I'm in a business much less hazardous than professional race-riding. In fact, I think in football you've got to be unlucky to be injured. If you go in for the ball honestly, without holding back, you'll very seldom get hurt.

The only injury which has put me out of the game for a while was one I got against Kilmarnock last season—and that was just bad luck.

It was a tackle from big Brian Rodman, and it was just a case of his mis-timing it.

I know it wasn't deliberate. For Brian and I are the best of pals. We come from the same part of Ayrshire. We've known each other since he was MY height!

Of course, any old-pals-act off the field goes right out the window the moment a match starts. It's too serious a game nowadays to be any different. Especially when at the end of the day it can mean a league championship or a cup.

Cooling down is something that doesn't take me very long. In fact, I've usually forgotten about a match half an hour after the finish.

There are times when I've gone home on a Saturday, had my wife ask me about the game—and found I couldn't remember who had scored. Apart from myself, that is.

Of course, when playing for Celtic, there are often a fair amount of goals to try to recall!

So, a little guy like me has his ups and downs, his serious and light-hearted moments. But one thing is for sure. I'll never get any bigger now.

So I'll never change my style. It's the only way I know how to play.

42

# A New Rising Star At Celtic Park

**W**ITH eight Scottish caps, five schoolboy and three junior, and an accent as broad as that of his boss, Jock Stein, it is a surprise to discover STEVE HANCOCK is, in fact, ENGLISH!

That's right, midfield man Steve was born in Sheffield—his father English, mother Scottish. He was only three months old when his parents brought him back north to his present home in Edinburgh.

Small but stockily built, Steve has all the makings of another "Stein Stunner".

Before joining up at Parkhead in the summer of 1971 he was Scotland's Junior Player of the Year with Newtongrange Star.

Already he's made a European Cup appearance for Celts' first team—against Sliema Wanderers in Malta.

Not bad going for an eighteen-year-old!

# FIVE-STAR

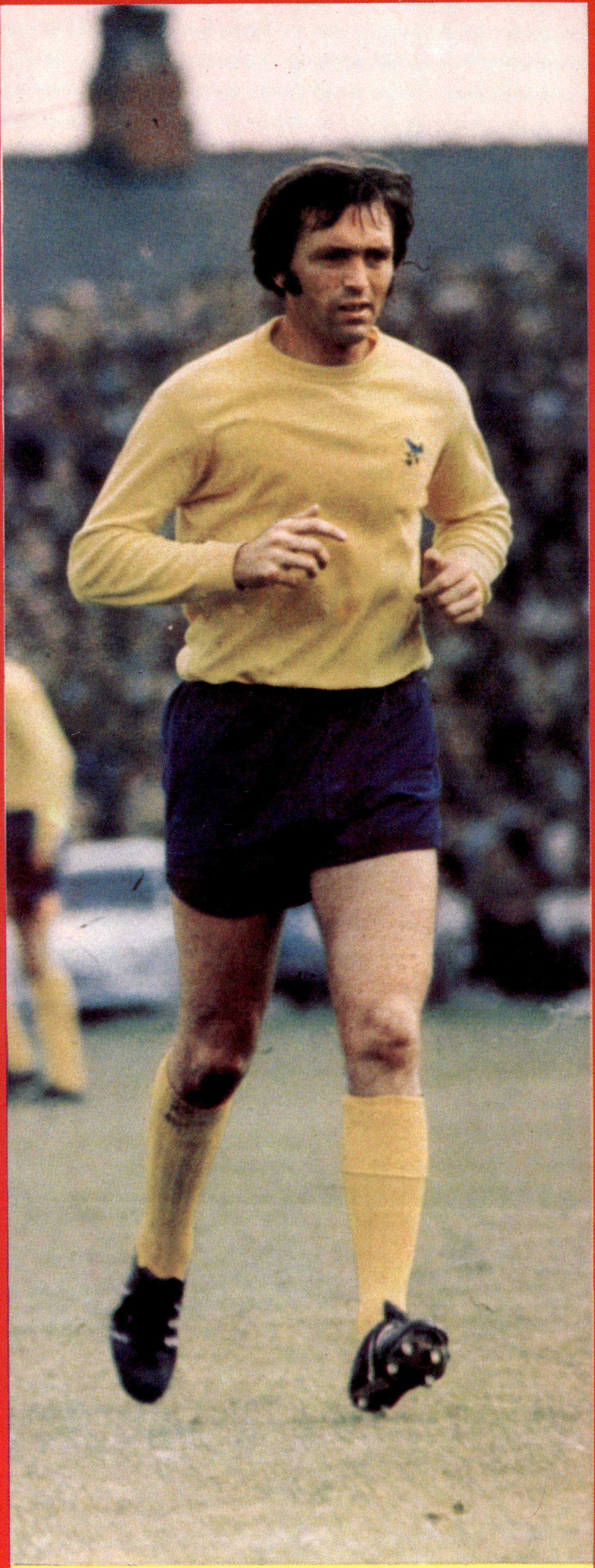

**JEFF ASTLE**
West Bromwich Albion

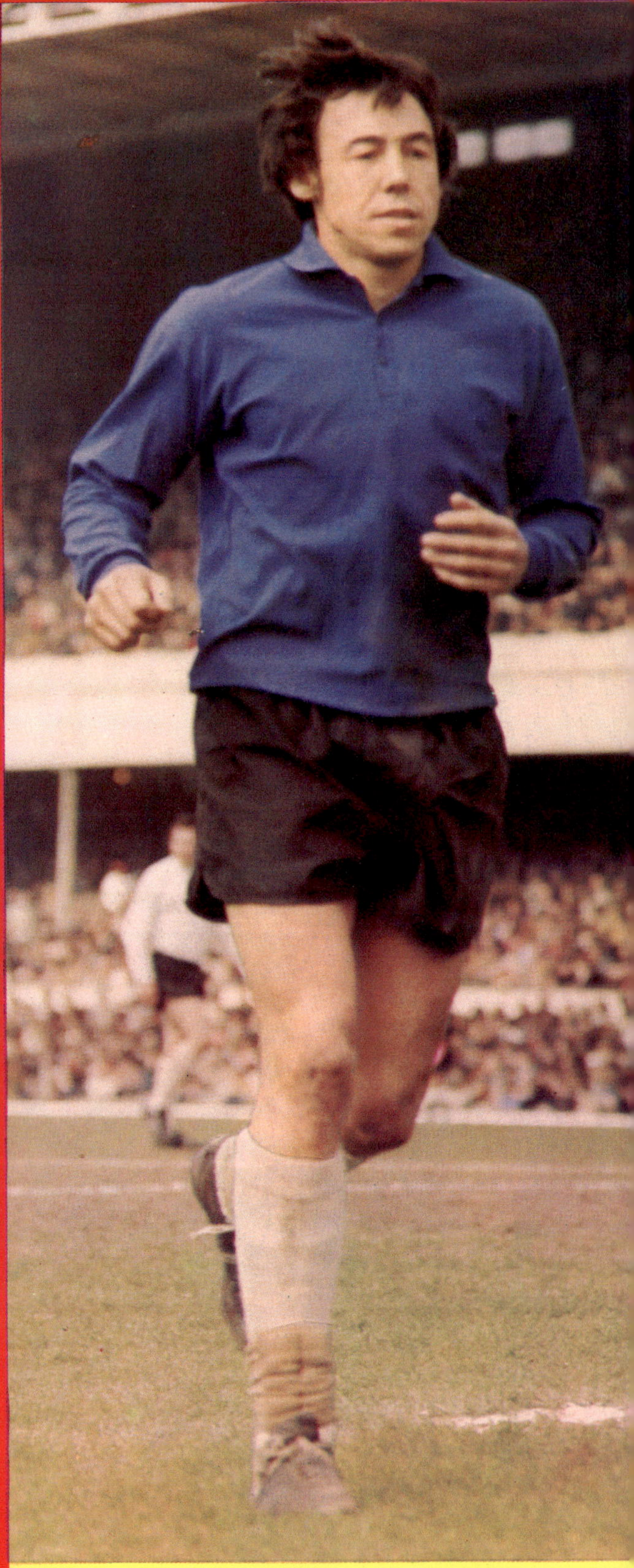

**GORDON BANKS**
Stoke City

# FOURSOME

**DAVID SADLER**
Manchester United

**CLYDE BEST**
West Ham United

**O**N the day John Connolly signed for the juvenile Glasgow United, his first "grown-up" club, United boss Andy Scott told him—"You'll be playing senior football within twelve months."

A somewhat reckless prediction, perhaps, but Andy was so convinced the fair-haired 16-year-old was a potential "great" that he had no qualms whatsoever.

**S**TAR players are discovered in so many different ways.

A lucky break while travelling around. A chance word in conversation. A hint in a county newspaper . . .

These are the sort of things that can lead talent-hunters to football aces in the raw.

As things turned out, his confidence was justified.

One night about six months later the phone rang in the Scott home. On the line was St Johnstone talent-spotter and former Scottish League referee, Alex. McClintock.

Andy was out of town on business, but his football-wise wife, Nancy, took the call. And she didn't hesitate when McClintock asked: "Does Andy have any worthwhile prospects at the moment?"

"He has several," she replied, "but the best of the lot is a boy called John Connolly. You're on a sure winner if you take him."

So Alex. McClintock, without having seen Connolly play, invited him to Perth for trials.

By the time he returned to Glasgow, John was a signed St Johnstone player.

"I was struck right away by the smoothness of his action and his beautiful ball control," recalls Saints' manager, Willie Ormond. "I didn't let him out of my sight until I had his name on a form."

St Johnstone sent a donation of £100 to Andy Scott's club.

At the end of the day they had made a profit of £74,900.

Because Everton paid £75,000 for Connolly.

*JOHN CONNOLLY*

## Dividend—From A Stroll In The Park

**I**T had been a disappointing night for Partick Thistle scout, Jimmy Dickie.

He'd travelled from his home to watch a highly-recommended West of Scotland amateur player—only to find the match postponed when he arrived at the ground.

Setting out for home once more, he chanced to stop his car to take a breath of fresh air in Glasgow's Knightswood Park.

That chance stopping was to change Jimmy's luck for the night—and produce for the "Jags" one of their biggest personalities in years in goalkeeper Alan Rough.

Alan was just a big, raw, 15-year-old school laddie, throwing himself around on the grass — stopping everything in an impromptu bounce match. But right away Jimmy sensed the boy's potential.

No sooner had the game finished and the jacket "goalposts" been lifted than he approached Alan. The big lad, who'd done a bit of 'keeping for his school, jumped at the scout's offer of training opportunities at Firhill.

From there he was farmed out to Sighthill Amateurs—finally being called up to help Thistle in their first ever season in the Second Division.

"I made a shaky start in the first team," says Alan. "But that was simply a case of having no real confidence in myself. But during that season I was picked for the Scottish Youth pool. That went a long way to boosting morale."

Within a few months of returning to the First Division Alan had won himself a League Cup Winners' medal and established himself as a favourite with the fans.

Now the boy who was picked up in a public park has his very own fan club, has gained further international honours, and is thought so highly of by his club they have turned down real big money for his transfer.

And all on account of a scout taking a stroll in the evening air. . . .

**T**HERE often happen quiet tips that allow a club to step in and make a headline signing before anyone else realises a player is available.

Arsenal had signed Alan Ball from Everton for £220,000 before any of the big spenders had an inkling he was available for transfer.

Spurs knew Arsenal were interested in Ralph Coates of Burnley. While the Gunners were

## SOFTLY, SOFTLY

tied up with the League and F.A. Cup double, they went to Burnley and paid a £190,000 fee.

Same when Derby County signed Colin Todd from Sunderland. While everyone else was weighing up the situation, Derby stepped in with a £170,000 bid that got the player.

Three cases of the tip-off that gave one club a head start on the rest of the field.

# TIP-OFF WORTH £75,000

## A Fascinating Letter in the Newspaper . . .

AS Manchester City has grown from being one of the also-ran clubs to winners of the League Championship, F.A. Cup, League Cup, European Cup-Winners' Cup and so on, a vital part of the " machine " has been wing-half Mike Doyle.

" And every time I see him play it reminds me to keep a close watch on the newspapers," says chief scout Harry Godwin.

Harry was a part-time spotter with City when, some years ago, he saw a letter in one of the newspapers around Manchester.

It said, in effect, " I'm not much good at school . . . I am going to be a P.E. teacher or a professional footballer when I grow up. Michael Doyle (aged 11), 10 Farley Way, Reddish, near Stockport."

" I stuck the cutting in my diary," Harry recalls. " Three years later I watched Stockport Boys play, and was immensely taken with the left back.

" I asked who he was, and was told — Michael Doyle.

" Where had I heard that name? I worried over it. Then, suddenly, I remembered.

" A frantic search for the old diary. Finding it, I was off right away to the address given in the paper. I knocked on the door — glanced through the window.

" On the table was a Manchester City programme. I have a chance here, I thought.

" When I got inside, first thing I saw was a policeman's helmet. I'll have to watch the moves now, I reckoned.

" Whatever, we got down to chatting — Mike's parents and me. And I found I had gone to school with his mother.

" I wasn't too surprised when we finally got him !

" Now, I keep looking for another clipping. . . ."

☆　☆　☆

## FRANK'S FREE NIGHT PAID OFF

BRENTFORD manager Frank Blunstone had a free night. He decided to go along and watch Southern League Wimbledon.

And there he saw a 6 ft. 3 in. centre-forward named John O'Mara. Without the grace of a Geoff Hurst or Martin Chivers, but big and strong and brave.

He decided to offer £750—and got himself a No. 9 who played a big part in Brentford climbing out of the Fourth Division last season. O'Mara also attracted £60,000 offers from other clubs.

☆　☆　☆

## Pat Stakes His Claim

ARSENAL'S Pat Rice supplied his own tip-off.

Belfast-born, Pat lived within a few minutes' walking distance of Highbury.

He turned up at the ground every Tuesday and Thursday evenings for youth training sessions — and was so enthusiastic he was given every encouragement.

Pat had a weak right foot. So he spent hours kicking the ball with that under-par member. Then he went all out to improve his heading ability.

" A lad like that just had to be given a chance," said manager Bertie Mee.

Peter was signed as an apprentice professional. Then a full-time professional. He became a member of the side that won the League and F.A. Cup double — and a regular for Ireland's national team.

But he still turns up at Highbury for a Sunday training session to try improve his game.

# RED FOR DANGER

Billy Bremner, Leeds United.

Willie Carr, Coventry City.

Jimmy Johnstone, Celtic.

Tommy Craig, Sheffield Wednesday.

**T**HESE four would stand out in any game. Not only for fiery hair—but because there's plenty fire about their play, too. When they're on the move—there's danger for the opposition.

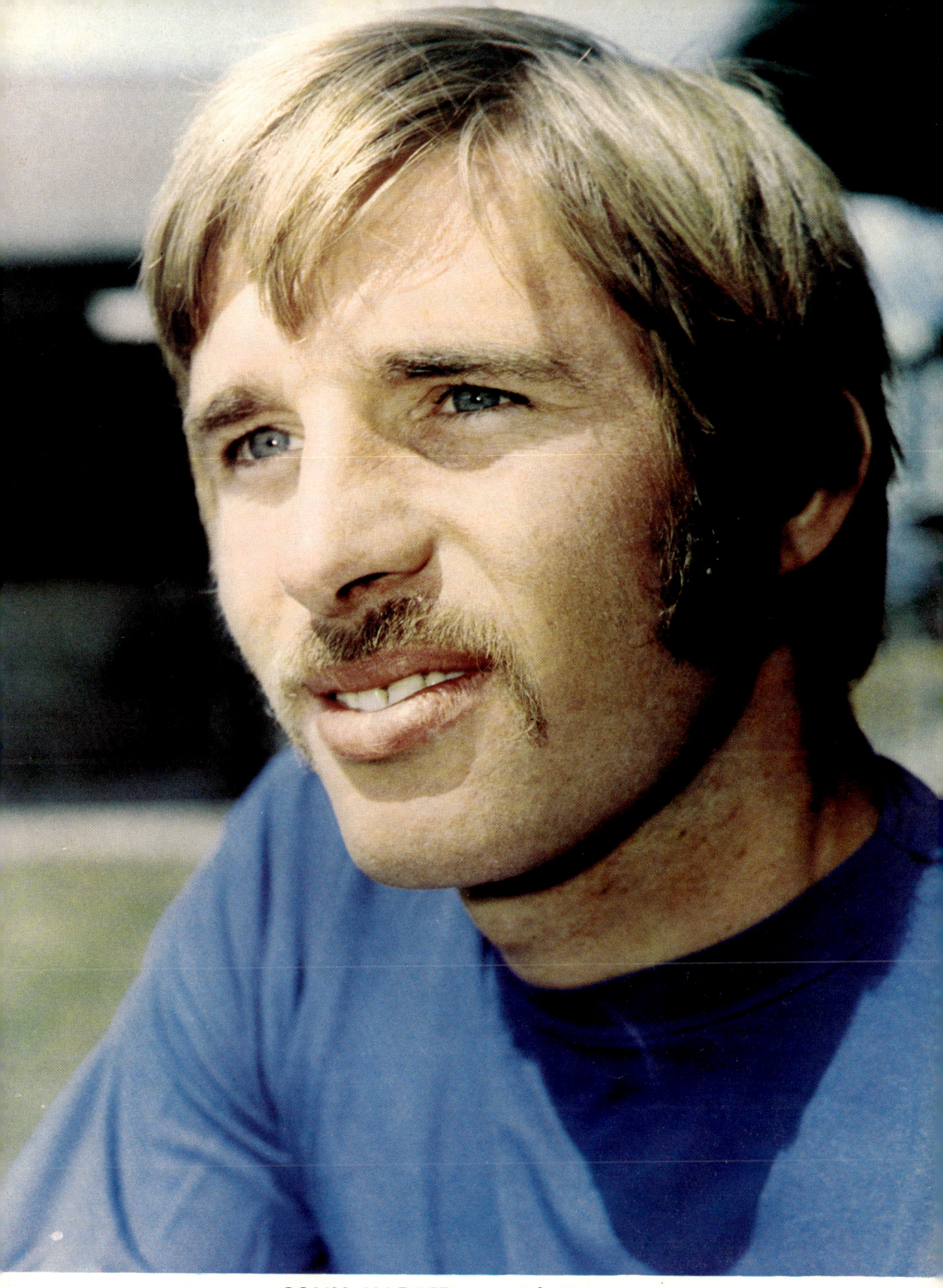

**COLIN HARPER, Ipswich Town**

49

**DEREK**

**JOHNSTONE**

*The real JOHN CHARLES — as he is today*

# A NEW "JOHN CHARLES"

## — But He's A Scot

"THE John Charles of the Seventies." The title fits 18-year-old Derek Johnstone of Glasgow Rangers.

Because, like the "Gentle Giant of Wales," this "Gentle Giant of Scotland" operates equally efficiently at centre-half or centre-forward.

Indeed, he goes one better by also doing a fair job in midfield. Any of Rangers' last season's European Cup Winners' Cup opponents will vouch for that. For it was the role he played in his club's home ties.

All in, last season for Derek can be broken down like this — centre-half away from home in Europe and also in Scottish Cup ties, mid-field in home European ties, centre-forward in League games.

## EPIC GOAL

Not bad going for this lad, who, after playing in only his second senior game, was thrust into the League Cup Final against the redoubtable Glasgow Celtic.

He headed the only goal of that game and was immediately hailed as Rangers' centre-forward for years to come. Now no one, least of all Derek himself, knows where he'll be playing.

It's a situation the big Dundonian isn't complaining about. He's delighted to get the chance to prove he can play anywhere. "It gives me more than one chance of a place in the team," he says.

Very soon now Derek is planning to set up business in his home town of Dundee. He has six brothers ready to help and to ensure it won't over-interfere with his football.

Not long after he joined Rangers, straight from school, Derek gave living in Glasgow a try. It lasted a week. Now he prefers the two-hour train journey between the two cities. Even although it means a 6.30 a.m. rise to make sure he's at Ibrox in time to start training at 10 prompt.

Before turning professional, he played for the Scotland Schoolboys Under-15 team. He was also a regular for St Francis Youth Club, the Dundee side who wear Celtic-type gear.

Although it's just a little over four years since he signed for Rangers, Derek has done a fair whack of travelling. His club's success in Europe assured that.

Indeed, he felt he'd had so much travelling by the end of last season that, instead of the normal footballer's Continental sunshine holiday, he spent a fortnight at the Aviemore Sports Centre with some friends.

Derek is an enthusiast for any ball game. Golf, tennis, badminton, table tennis, snooker. You name it. And he's good at them all.

He's pretty good at family relations, too . . .

As soon as Rangers won their place in the European Cup-winners' final, all players were told they could take wives, girl friends or friends to Barcelona for the big show.

While the team carried out their preparations in a special training camp, the guests would enjoy themselves at a nearby holiday resort.

And, of course, best-seat tickets would be laid on for "the night."

Right away Derek decided — he'd take his widowed mother.

"Mum comes first in my book," he says.

# STRIPE

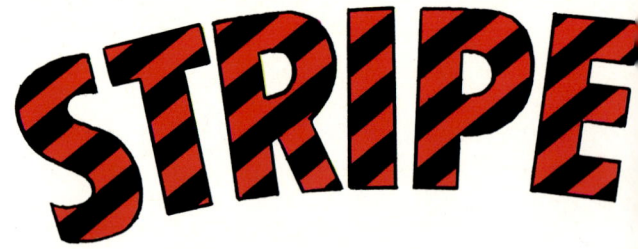

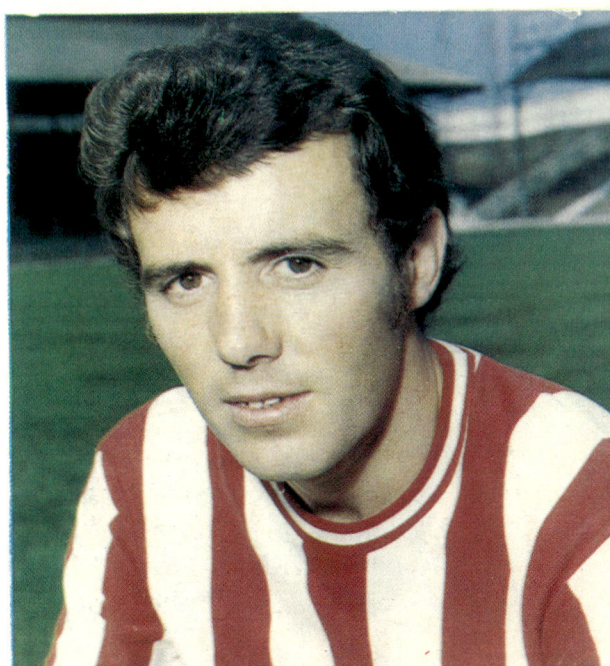

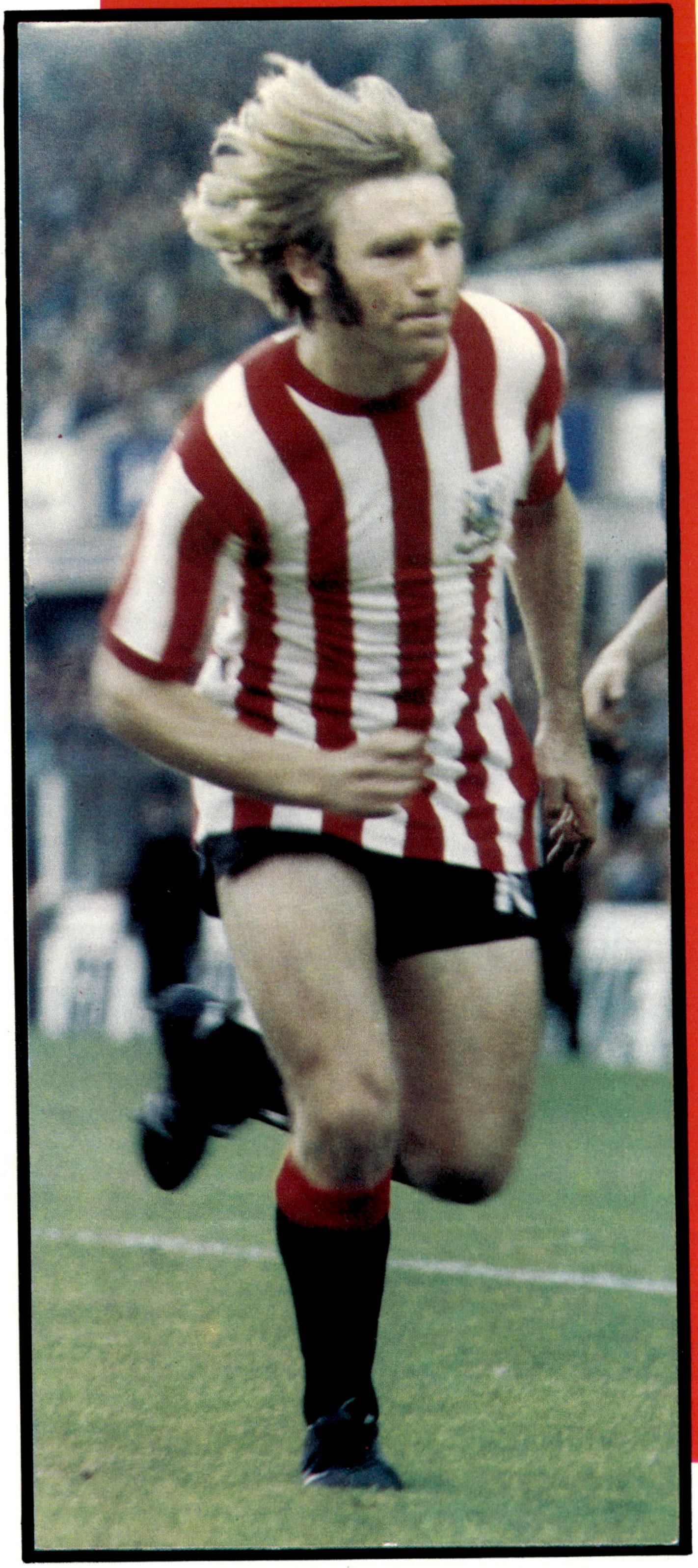

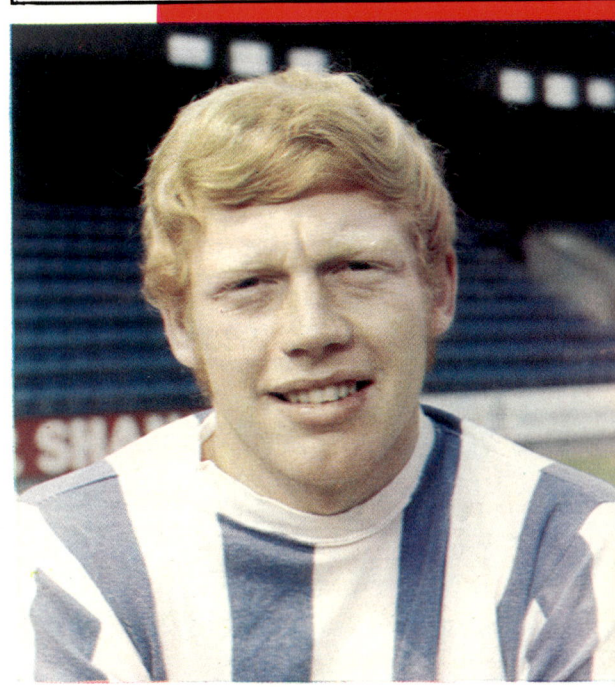

TONY CURRIE
Sheffield United

JOHN DOCHERTY
Brentford

GEOFF HUTT
Huddersfield Town

# STRIPS

**DAVID CLEMENT**
**Queens Park Rangers**

**LEN CANTELLO**
**West Bromwich Albion**

**MALCOLM MACDONALD**
**Newcastle United**

# TALL ORDER FOR

I CANNOT really remember when first I got the urge to score goals.

It must have been born in me — because I don't recall NOT having it.

In football I love to be in the thick of things. And, because the whole object of the exercise is to stick the ball in the net, there is no one happier than me when I'm doing just that . . . regularly.

Not to put too fine a point on it, I'm a bit of a glory hunter. I admit that.

Of course, the urge to score and the opportunity at higher levels isn't the same thing.

The opportunity came at Fulham. So many injuries cropped up that I, generally recognised as a full-back there, was pushed into the forward line.

And I scored goals. Then moved on to Luton Town as a now recognised scorer.

I cracked home 28 goals in my first season at Kenilworth Road.

Second season there, Manager Alex Stock said, "You have a target for this season. 45 goals."

When a couple of dozen is regarded, nowadays, as top-flight scoring power, that was quite an assignment.

Like I say, though, I believe in myself. By halfway through I'd knocked in 21. It went a bit quieter after that, but I still managed 30.

That isn't bad by any standards, even if not 45. Which I don't think the boss really expected in the first place!

Of course, the great breakthrough came with my transfer to Newcastle United. To the First Division.

I know a lot of people wondered if I'd do it up there. I think 30 goals (23 League, two F.A. Cup, one League Cup and four Texaco Cup) in my first season proved I can.

Y'know, I don't worry about opponents.

I don't go out there thinking, "Oh, it's him against me today. He's a great player."

What I believe in is not the "I hope I can do it" attitude, but the "I KNOW I can do it" approach.

Not taken to stupid extremes, of course.

For instance, if I find the fellow I'm against is winning in the air, I get the ball on the ground.

That's commonsense.

I consider myself an extremely limited player as far as some of the skills go. I have strengths and weaknesses.

Of course, I train to improve these weaknesses but I don't let them worry me at all. Instead, I concentrate on the strengths — speed, the ability to take the ball

**Power in the header**          **Left-foot venom**

By
# MALCOLM MACDONALD
### Newcastle United

round the keeper and keep a cool head in tight situations.

Actually, I'm improving in the skills, too, with playing in a higher class of football.

But I still feel I lack a touch of stamina. Not the stamina (mental) to concentrate throughout a game but the stamina (physical) to run and work all the time.

I don't think I need to say I'm very, very ambitious in the game.

I've been disappointed since I was 14 every time I've seen an England team named. I've thought — why can't I be one of them? It has eased a bit since I got the first of my Under-23 honours last season! Then there were these other recognitions that came along . . .

# A TALL SCORER

*It's a goal!*                    *Point of order*

But what I'd really like to do is win a World Cup winners' medal with England — to put alongside all sorts of club honours with Newcastle.

Wouldn't that really be something?

Yes, goals are my business. I love talking about them and scoring them.

But I don't (1) have a best or a worst goal I've ever scored, and don't (2) have a hero.

On the first point, I believe even if the ball goes in off your backside it's a good goal. It follows logically that I'll never score a bad one!

I don't have a hero, but I believe, as a scorer myself, that Jimmy Greaves was in a class of his own.

I'll line up Denis Law as well. Which doesn't knock Denis, but shows that, even by talking about him in the same paragraph as Jimmy, I rate him, too.

Jimmy would choose a square foot of the penalty area to go into in the certain knowledge that the ball would end up there and be "made" for him tucking it away in the net. He was so cool.

It was my kind of magic . . .

## Mile Upon Mile For Plymouth Argyle

FOOTBALL is now a world game. Clubs think nothing about boarding a plane and playing matches at the furthest ends of Europe — or the world for that matter!

But few can clock up more miles than Plymouth Argyle. Some 12,000 each season for away matches.

Argyle pretty well consider Bristol Rovers (120 miles away) and Bournemouth (122 miles) as local "derby" matches. They lost their one really local match when Torquay (32 miles) were relegated to Division Four last season.

One man who knows all about the travels of Plymouth is manager Ellis Stuttard. He joined up at Home Park in 1938 as a hard-tackling wing-half from Burnley. He has had spells elsewhere at places like Exeter and Swindon, at one time scouting for Arsenal. But always he seems to go back to Argyle.

"I feel like I have covered a million miles since I moved to Devon," says Mr Stuttard. "Yet I've never regretted one of them.

"This season we have new fixtures we regard as 'local' — against Charlton, Brentford, Watford and Southend. We also have Grimsby and Scunthorpe that present much more in the way of travel. But it all works out."

### "CHICKEN-FEED"

For long-distance matches, Plymouth travel by coach. Starting out very early Friday morning. Seldom arriving back in Plymouth until 1 or 2 a.m. on Sunday morning.

"The players get used to it," says Mr Stuttard. "No one ever seems to get fed up. There is always a game of cards and a natter to keep us occupied. We regard a 100-mile trip as chicken-feed."

A big problem as far as the Argyle are concerned is to get players to move to the West Country.

"They look at the map and contemplate the borders of Cornwall," says Mr Stuttard. "That seems an awful long way from Manchester, London and Birmingham. It means the West Country has got to be sold to them. But, once they get here, they seldom want to go back."

**TERRY CONROY, Stoke City**

# CUP COUP

**I**T was my first game at Wembley. Also my team's first Wembley appearance.

High in the stand were 52 of my relatives – watching me in the League Cup Final. For many of them it was first time in England.

It was Stoke versus Chelsea.

Just in case you don't know, let me tell you Stoke have been members of the Football League for 108 years and had never won any major trophy up to this Wembley day in March this year.

That is a LONG, LONG, LONG time to have an empty silverware cupboard.

So here we were at Wembley . . . with a team mixture of fantastic experience (in George Eastham, Gordon Banks and Peter Dobing), and bouncy, happy, willing youngsters like Mike Bernard, Denis Smith, John

**By**

# TERRY CONROY

## Stoke City

Mahoney, our two young full backs, Pejic and Marsh — and myself, of course.

But Chelsea were everyone's favourites. The bookies had them odds on. And 90 per cent. of the professionals in the game gave us little chance.

Well, we gave them a fright in just 4 minutes 40 seconds ! That is how long it took us to score. I did it—though I really could not believe that I had.

It went like this . . .

Peter Dobing sent over a very long throw-in. Peter Bonetti punched out. George Eastham flighted it back into the box. Denis Smith shot—and the ball was deflected in a curve through the air.

Instinctively I leapt and headed past Bonetti. When I saw the ball in the back of the net I immediately looked at the referee. Then I looked at the linesman . . . then I looked at the ref. again.

For, every time I net with my head, it seems I'm offside, or somebody has fouled the 'keeper, or . . .

But the ref. seemed satisfied this time. And, as the lads closed in on me with elation all over their faces—I knew all was well.

If that goal boosted our morale, it didn't half get Chelsea going. They rammed into us—with Cooke, Hudson and Hollins taking a mighty grip in midfield. By half-time Peter Osgood had grabbed an equaliser and we were right under the collar.

Then, in a pulsating second half, we got going again. And our winning goal was scored by the man everybody in the country wanted to see on the winners' side.

George Eastham, 35 years old, a player with almost as many admirers as Bobby Charlton. He shot home the winner.

I centred after a long run down the left wing. Big John Ritchie headed down to Jimmy Greenhoff—whose first-time shot was knocked out by Bonetti. George, cool as you like, told Peter Dobing to get out of the way—and then poked the ball home.

A wonderful player had helped Stoke win their first cup in 108 years. Only because of the referee clamp-down was he back with us after going to South Africa to manage Hellenic.

When that was imposed our manager, Tony Waddington, felt the climate of the game was ideal for George. So he asked him to come back.

Up the famous Wembley stairways I went, then, to collect my first English medal. Thanks a little to George — but even more to his dad, George Eastham, Senior.

How did I come to be there? Me, a Dublin lad who played hurling and Gaelic football as a kid before turning to football.

I first played for the famous Home Farm club in Dublin—in the under 13, 14, 15, 16 and 17 teams. But I was no eyecatcher. Plenty club scouts from English clubs came to watch us, but nobody ever asked about me. Maybe that wasn't surprising. I was SO tiny it was unbelievable. A regular midget.

But, at 17 years of age, things changed for me. I shot up six inches. The senior team at Home Farm scooped all the cups, leagues and trophies we played for—and Glentoran, the Belfast club, signed me.

I had been with them three months when Newcastle started to watch me regularly.

Then Fulham came and asked me to sign. And Stoke City began to take interest.

Unknown to me, I had two champions. George Eastham senior and Mr John Keenan, a cattle dealer from Dublin.

Mr Keenan had watched me at Home Farm—and sometimes with Glentoran. He was in England almost every week on business and had become a close personal friend of manager Waddington of Stoke. He kept insisting I must be signed.

Anyway, after a lot of persuading by Mr Keenan and Mr Eastham, Tony Waddington came over to watch me play for Glentoran. Then we met on the train from Belfast to Dublin as I travelled home.

After that journey I decided to sign for Stoke—mainly because I could not help feeling it would be wonderful to work for Waddington. I was right, too.

I made my debut for the first team against Leicester at home. We won 3-2, and I scored a goal. That was a good start. But it didn't help me overcome my biggest problem. I was scared to make a mistake.

## TURNING POINT

It took me two years to get over that. In that first season I played 10 games. Most of them very cautiously. So cautiously that the end of the season might easily have seen the parting of the ways between me and Stoke.

At the start of the following season I was facing the reality of my position. WAS I GOOD ENOUGH FOR THE FIRST DIVISION?

We played two pre-season friendlies against Oldham and Plymouth, both Fourth Division sides then. And in the dressing-room before the first match against Oldham I made the decision I am convinced set me on the right road to a secure future.

I said to myself, " I can do anything I want against the defenders of a Fourth Division club. Surely I can? If I can't, I might as well face reality. That I am not good enough."

I let myself go and had a wonderful game. I did the same against Plymouth. Another cracking game.

These may seem like trivial little points to you. But those, I am convinced, were the two games that made it possible for me to go forward with new heart. I've never really looked back — except for two cartilage operations.

Naturally, my free-running style exposes my rather slim frame to all sorts of mistimed tackles and associated knocks. But I don't mind that. What I can't stand is defenders who set out to do me damage. Yes, they're around . . .

**THE**

ALF STAN
Partick Thistl
— in his ol
Q.P. jerse

# BIG BOY CLUB

**I**T'S exclusive — HIGHLY exclusive.

Membership only for league footballers whose height is not less than 6ft. 2in.

And what a formidable looking team of giants such a company could field.

Maybe not all filling normal positions, but lining-up this way —
CORRIGAN, Manchester City (6 ft. 4 in.); YOUNG, Aberdeen (6 ft. 3 in.); KEARNS, Oxford United (6 ft. 3 in.); ATKINS, Halifax Town (6 ft. 2½ in.); CHARLTON, Leeds United (6 ft. 2½ in.); TAYLOR, Bristol Rovers (6 ft. 4 in.); STAMP, Partick Thistle (6 ft. 5 in.); DOUGAN, Wolves (6 ft. 3 in.); CHIVERS, Spurs (6 ft. 2½ in.); O'MARA, Brentford (6 ft. 3 in.); WADDLE, Halifax Town (6 ft. 3 in.). Subs.— KINNEAR, Hearts (6 ft. 3 in.); MOORE, Southend United (6 ft. 2 in.); PARKES, Wolves (6 ft. 3 in.).

Now, if only Scotland's Tom Wharton (6 ft. 3 in. and 15 stone) would come out of retirement to referee any game this lot might play, there could be a situation like happened in a Scottish First Division match some years ago.

## VALUE FOR MONEY

Airdrie were playing Kilmarnock. Doug Baillie (6 ft. 3 in. and 14½ stone), the Airdrie captain, tossed for ends with Killie's Jimmy Brown (6 ft. and 14 stone). The referee was Mr Wharton.

" Here was probably the biggest and heaviest trio ever to appear in a centre circle — anywhere," says Baillie, who now writes about football instead of playing it.

The thought obviously occurred to referee Wharton at the time.

He told the two skippers — " If there's a break-in here today we should be able to sort them out personally."

Of course, no " Big Boys' Club " of today could hope to have on its membership list a superman like you see on the right.

He is Willie Foulke, who was Chelsea's goalkeeper-captain at the turn of this century.

Despite his 6 ft. 3 in. frame carried 22 st. 3 lb. — only a pound less than both his backs put together — Foulke's agility was astounding.

He was capped by England, picked up two Cup-winners' medals — and also played cricket for Derbyshire, his native county.

Sheffield United made Foulke a senior. They paid £19 for him from a Derbyshire colliery club.

Which, if only on point of weight, was an outstanding value-for-money deal.

WILLIE FOULKE
*Chelsea*

## From Life In A Monastery To "Thumbing Around The Continent"

LEARNING to be a REAL PROFESSIONAL footballer took me a long time. Almost too long.

I was a sensation with Celtic at first. Then a flop.

And I have had my ups and downs with my present club, Aston Villa.

My trouble has been that I never really knew what I wanted to do with my life. I reckon that is what makes me different from most lads in the game today.

At Villa Park they call me "The Hippie." And, at that, I reckon I am a bit of an odd-ball.

Last summer, while the rest of my team mates sunned themselves on the Costa Bravas of the Mediterranean, I hitch-hiked across Austria with a rucksack on my back.

Of course, with Villa winning promotion, I got a good big bonus pay-out. I also get well paid at Villa Park.

I could easily have booked a luxurious hotel and tasted the sweet life. But I like to do different things. That way much more can be experienced.

I suppose this different approach to life has come about because of the way I grew up and came in and out of the game before settling down with Aston Villa.

You see, I spent seven years studying to become a priest. I played very little football in those years . . . from 12 years old until 19.

But I always liked to go behind the monastery and juggle with a football

Then suddenly, when I was 19, I decided to end my studies for the priesthood. Naturally my parents were disappointed. Everybody felt I had failed.

I did not think so, but in order to get away from people who were a little disappointed, I decided to hitch-hike round Europe.

I took a guitar and headed for the Continent. I slept in hostels and sometimes fields. Just thumbing my way around.

When I got back to Britain I worked as a navvy on the building sites for some months. At that stage I never thought for a second that I would become a top footballer.

Then I started to play centre-forward for Kilsyth Rangers, the Scottish junior club. I had all the skills, but was not particularly aggressive. It was just a pastime to me.

Then I took a job in London with the Post Office. I went and lived down there in a flat.

# THE DAY I GOT THE MESSAGE

## By PAT McMAHON
### Aston Villa

Naturally I stopped playing for Kilsyth Rangers.

But then, purely by accident, I was thrown into the limelight in Kilsyth's Junior Cup-winning year.

Drew Jarvie, now with Aberdeen but then with Kilsyth, was badly injured at the start of the team's cup run.

The club officials got in touch with me. Would I fly up for every cup-tie? They would pay for the flight.

I agreed to do my stuff. And, because of the run right through to the final, professional clubs began to take notice of me.

Right out of the blue, Celtic came for me. I was always Celtic daft. I jumped at the chance and signed. They had just won the European Cup.

In my first season at Celtic Park I was in the first team. And played well, too.

Suddenly, Jock Stein put me in the reserves. I reacted the wrong way. I stopped playing.

That is where I discovered that you can't do that in professional football. So I stayed in the reserves for most of the second year at Parkhead.

I thought I was too good for the reserves. I expected I would get back into the first team when somebody in the forward line lost form.

But all Jock Stein did was pick somebody who was playing well in the reserve side.

Jock didn't like my attitude — and told me so. I argued with him. I didn't know any better then.

I hadn't been schooled in the game. Really, I didn't know what it was all about.

At the end of the season I was given a free transfer. But I was back in the game quickly.

Tommy Docherty was the new manager of Aston Villa. He told me, "I think you can play a bit. But I AM taking a risk. I'm willing to back my judgment if you are willing to work at the game."

But although I got into the first team I never really developed the right attitude. I still thought of Saturday afternoon as a bit of fun.

The "Doc" kept hammering away at me. I was played as a striker, but I didn't like being up the front all the time.

When Vic Crowe took over, I found, for the first time, I was with a manager who talks quietly.

Immediately he made me a midfield player.

He took me into his office one day for the longest face-to-face talk I have ever had.

He got straight down to cases—"What you lack almost completely is any competitiveness. Out on the pitch you do not try to win the ball AT ALL!

"You do not seem to realise the ball has to be won. So do the games.

"To play brilliantly when you have the ball is not enough. You have to play off the ball and try to win the ball."

In a pre-season friendly against Birmingham City I had one job to do. WIN THE BALL! I did it, too.

That, I believe, was the turning point for me.

# CUP TOURNEY THAT

**I**T'S the cup competition to beat the band.

It has only three entrants — but will take five years to complete.

It involves two teams from Britain — and one outwith the country.

It was started in 1968 — but its fine new trophy has still to be won.

And it may not be competed for again — due to the heavy costs involved.

It's the North Atlantic Cup — competed for by teams from three groups of islands away far north from the mainland of Scotland.

The Orkneys, the Shetlands and the Faroes — once a Danish possession but now independent.

They're keen on their football in these outposts. Inter-island games have gone on for long enough.

But, four years ago, after a match in the Faroese capital of Thorshavn, the three island associations decided to start a new competition.

Appropriately, it was called "The North Atlantic Cup Tournament" — to be run on a league basis, with each team playing two home and two away games against each other.

When the match schedule was drawn up, travel expenses were kept very much in mind.

Because, with no regular steamer or air service, charter aircraft would be necessary. And that's a costly business. Around £1000 a flight.

There was also the matter of weather to consider.

Due to gales, heavy rainfall and long hours of darkness falling shortly after 3 p.m. each day, football is practically impossible in these parts from October to April.

So, when all was said and done, it was found this show just had to be stretched out to five years.

Completion will be reached next summer — when the Faroese will make the 200-mile flight south to play in the Orkneys and Shetlands.

*" Am I still in time for the kick-off?
I fell off the boat —"*

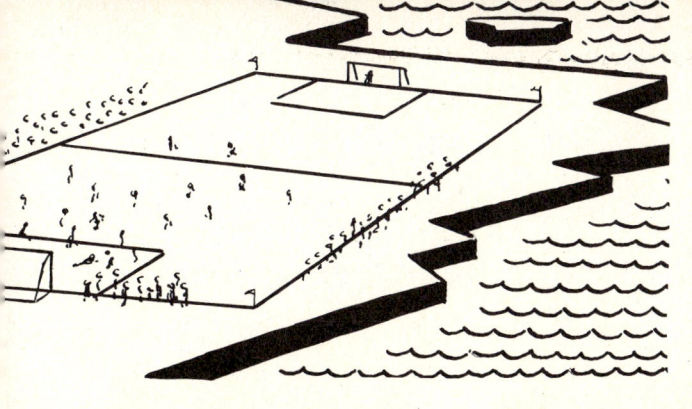

# LASTS FOR 5 YEARS

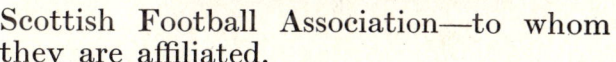

They'll bring a few fans, too—but nothing like what used to be when cheaper sea transport was available.

There was even a year in which the Faroes team and a batch of supporters made passage to the Shetlands by fishing boat—bucking grey and angry seas for more than 24 hours.

Due to intervals between games, North Atlantic Cup results are sometimes forgotten by fans. And officials themselves have to keep on checking the records.

But, forecast is that, when the series of 12 games is at an end, the Faroes team will be out in front.

Among the shop assistants, Civil servants, farmers and builders who so enthusiastically take part in the tournament, this most northerly territory seems to have the best players among their population of 35,000.

Club football is spread well over the islands. And there are many significant names. Both from towns and country.

Like Lerwick Celtic and Lerwick Rangers—and Kirkwall Hotspur. Plus Stromness, Scalloway and South Ronaldsay.

There is a fine Viking sound, too, about the names of the towns from which come the Faroes clubs—Thorshavn, Klaksvik and Vagaa.

Quite often the Orkneys and Shetlands have a coach sent them by the Scottish Football Association—to whom they are affiliated.

Recently, too, the S.F.A. sent £500 to help finances. But, mostly, cash is raised by dances, raffles and prize draws.

It is indeed a big moment when a visit is made by a Scottish League team—or a side from the not so distant Highland League.

That really pulls out the crowds. Though, in the first North Atlantic Cup tie, on Thorshavn's cinder-track pitch, a most respectable 4000 turned up. They paid ten kroners each, too. That's 50p.

Up to now, no British league club has taken a player from 'way up there.

But, in the Cup rounds of 1970, Orkney goalkeeper Harcus put up a show against Faroes that is still talked about as good enough for any club in the business.

This was a game hit by the fog that so often takes these islands in its grip.

Once only the intervention of the local Member of Parliament got the Orkney team a plane home after three days' wait.

**A**WAY at the other end of the pitch, the cameraman presses his shutter-button —and up comes this revealing back view of a penalty kick.

A perfect conversion it is, too— by JIMMY GABRIEL (Southampton) v. West Ham.

See how Gabriel (No. 5) has "foxed" goalkeeper BOBBY FERGUSON into diving right—while the ball is shot powerfully SO far away into the other corner of the net.

Almost as if these supporters' scarves had been used as leading marks.

Watching it all happen is JOHN McDOWELL of the "Hammers"—and these participants are also shown front view — top—FERGUSON; Bottom left—GABRIEL, and bottom right—McDOWELL.

# PENALTY!
## CLOSE-UP *from* LONG-RANGE

# These Names Spell **ACTION**

## Picture lines by... **DEREK DOUGAN** (WOLVES)
He knows them all . . .

# Wyn Davies, **MANCHESTER CITY**

THIS is a typical action shot of the big Welshman. Always in the place where it really hurts . . . the penalty box. His scars — he's had 119 stitches during his career, I believe — testify to that.

Wyn's work in the box last season made Francis Lee City's record goalscorer since the war.

Notice Lee, poised right there on his left, ready for the break of the ball.

# Peter Lorimer, LEEDS UTD.

**WHAT** a picture! Sums up everything about Peter Lorimer—AND the reason it's so tough to score goals against Liverpool.

Emlyn Hughes, Larry Lloyd and John Toshack surround the Leeds man. They are giving him special attention. But, and this is Lorimer's strength, despite being hemmed in, he gives everything to his shot. He reminds me so much of my boyhood hero—" **THE CANNONBALL KID.**"

# Phil Parkes, WOLVES

JUST imagine trying to beat THAT goalkeeper to the ball! A giant of a man with a giant heart.

He is, of course, my team-mate. But, with improvement in concentration and confidence, he would immediately be in the country's top four.

Also notice that wonderful Leeds striker, Mick Jones. Right up in the air to give maximum of challenge to the 'keeper.

And look where our Bernard Shaw is. Covering on the line. He clears more balls there than any full-back in the league.

# Dave Webb, CHELSEA

FOUR Chelsea stalwarts . . . defending their line. That's why goals are hard to come by these days.

Peter Bonnetti (on the right) is a well-beaten 'keeper. But there are three Chelsea men on blocking duty.

And it is no surprise to me that the ball is being cleared by David Webb, one of the London side's strong men. Behind him Paddy Mulligan and Peter Osgood form a solid wall.

# Mike England, SPURS

THE under-dog here is Neil Martin of Nottingham Forest. And I'll say —
Neil, old pal, I know what it's like. Mike England knows all the answers about getting up in the air for the ball — and keeping an opponent down.

Mike, a colleague of mine with Blackburn Rovers a few years back, is one of the most astute centre-halves in the business. He can be ruthless at times. This picture shows that. But, either way, he is difficult to beat.

WELCOME HOME NOBBY

IT was a famous day when NOBBY STILES came back to Old Trafford to play for Middlesbrough in last season's F.A. Cup.

A hug from DENIS LAW

An exit with GEORGE BEST

A parting salute from LAW — with ALE STEPNEY coming up to add his congrats

# ALL SET TO CLINCH A PLACE IN BIG-TIME

**M**OST young players are full of expectations for the future. Once signed by a big club they are inclined to think they are almost there.

But young IRVING NATTRASS saw things a little differently. After a year on the apprentice list with Newcastle he felt he was a total failure.

He says, "I made up my mind to quit. I started to look round for a job."

That would have been a calamity. For this fellow has all the qualities needed to make the grade. He has already had several first team outings.

Filling in during skipper Bobby Moncur's absence, he was suddenly confronted with the job of stopping some of the finest strikers in the game.

Moncur says of him, "Definitely one for the future. He is inclined to get easily depressed with his progress. If only he rated himself as highly as the rest of the senior players do."

This former Ferryhill Grammar School kid will make it . . . despite his occasional doubts.

**A** YOUNG star with Manchester United can have a lot "going for him"—and a lot "going against him"!

Vouching for that is inside-forward SAMMY McILROY, the Manchester United lad whose admirers include George Best, Bobby Charlton, Denis Law and Sir Matt Busby.

*The player behind Nattrass is IAN MELLOR, Manchester City*

# CHALLENGE AHEAD FOR THE BOY FROM BELFAST

**SAMMY McILROY, Manchester United**

**BOBBY PARKER**
**Coventry City**

**DAVID SUNLEY**
**Sheffield Wednesday**

MARK down BOBBY PARKER as the youngster most likely to get the Bobby Moore position with England in about four years' time.

Yes, the Coventry defender is THAT good! He has played several times for the England Youth side — and captained them to the mini World Youth Championship in Czechoslovakia.

At 19 he has already been selected by Sir Alf Ramsey as sub for the England Under-23 team.

Says Bob Dennison, chief scout at Coventry — "He has got the lot. He is undoubtedly the young British player who most resembles Moore in style and temperament."

MANAGERS far from Sheffield often mention DAVID SUNLEY. They say this full-back has a big future in the game.

Because he is tough, fast and one of the most competitive players at Hillsborough.

Born in the Yorkshire village of Skelton, he went straight to Wednesday when 15.

His influence and impact in the youth team was dramatic. He helped them to the final of the Northern Intermediate Cup three seasons in succession — though they lost all three finals.

Those were disappointments to Sunley. As was his fortnight's suspension for three bookings and the crippling leg injury suffered at the start of last season in a friendly match.

But he has shown the character to overcome these set-backs and could go on to become as famous a defender as was Ron Staniforth, the man who now coaches him.

GEORGE ANDERSON, Greenock Morton, is destined to become one of the biggest names in Scottish football — and maybe English, too, in time.

He has a lot to thank his father for. Dad is very much George's own personal manager. The relationship is almost like that of boxing manager and his brightest prospect.

That's "for" him. Against him is the tremendous pressure exerted from outside the game.

Agents rush to sign him up for lucrative business interests. People who want him around them all the time. Invitations flow regularly. The adulation is intense.

These are the dangers Sammy must surmount if he is to go right to the top.

This Belfast lad says, "My father told me he did not want to hear any stories about me in night clubs or any off-the-field goings-on!

"The most I would want off the field is a little sports shop."

McIlroy has broken through into the first team. His real challenge comes when he tries to emulate such "greats" as Best, Charlton and Law.

They say he will. He says he is keeping his feet on the ground.

# COVENTRY "KID" WITH THE BOBBY MOORE TOUCH

Left to right —

★ GEORGE ANDERSON
Morton

★ TERRY LEE
Spurs

★ PAUL HARRIS
Orient

"He won't be rushed. He'll prepare for a career outside the game — just in case," says Mr Anderson. And with George in complete agreement, that's just the way this young centre-half's life is taking shape.

He's training to be an accountant.

"With an accountancy degree behind me, I'll know how to use the money I make out of football," he says.

Owner of a string of Youth caps, it seems only a matter of time till George adds big honours to the list. For Scottish team manager Tommy Docherty considers him "one of the best boys in the game at present."

MIKE BUCKLEY
Everton

EVERTON chief scout, Harry Cook, pulled off something special when he brought MIKE BUCKLEY from Manchester to Everton. He had to fend off both Manchester United and Manchester City.

That was three years ago. Now, says Harry — "Mike is proving it was all worth while. He had played for England Schoolboys several times. Although small, he clearly had the ability.

"He has shown his worth in the first team. He is a bit like Johnny Giles, but can tackle better.

"He may not have Giles's flair yet, but he uses the ball well and is a fine positional player.

"Definitely one who has progressed as we hoped. He looks likely to go on and on, getting better and better."

THE fellow with the job of understudying 'keeper Pat Jennings of Spurs is 20-year-old TERRY LEE.

5 ft. 11 in., agile and sure, he is the right age to develop and eventually succeed the Irishman.

Stepney-born Terry came to Spurs via New Zealand. When he emigrated to that country in 1964, he was a mid-field player — good enough to take part in a schoolboy international trial.

He returned to England to live at Hornchurch, and played as a goalkeeper for Havering and Essex County Boys' teams.

Signed for Spurs as an apprentice in April, 1968. Became a fully-fledged professional in May, 1970.

ORIENT have a reputation for producing top young centre-halves.

There was Paul Went, for whom Charlton paid £27,500, and Tommy Taylor, a £90,000 "sell" to West Ham. Now they have PAUL HARRIS.

He made the breakthrough last season, in Orient's cup run, when he dealt firmly with players like Alan Birchenall, Peter Osgood and Ray Kennedy.

"I learned a lot from our cup matches," says Harris. "Particularly from a player like Osgood, who is always tempting you to commit yourself. I'm much better at waiting for my chance these days."

Tall and fair-haired and still only 19, Paul Harris looks a "natural" for a big future.

**LEN GLOVER, Leicester City**

# A Switch —And Terry Struck It Rich

ON REVIE must still break out in a cold eat when he thinks that, ur or five years ago, he de outside-left TERRY OOPER available for nsfer.

t is also reported the fee nted was a mere £10,000!

The key, of course, is the scription "outside-left." at's what Terry was at and Road—and, frankly, t all that hot a winger.

Came a switch to full-back the reserves—and a amatic rise to world class.

Terry came good as a full-ck at precisely the time in tball history when the rrel - chested, billiards - le - legged Nos. 2 and 3 re on the way out.

Because of the 4-3-3 for-ation in particular, full-cks had not only to win e ball, they had to use the ng space in front of them create attacks.

Terry was custom-built the job.

He has pace — especially e acceleration so vital to yone in the top flight.

He has ball control and bbling ability, which in-eased in direct ratio to owing confidence as first eds, then England, made an automatic choice.

He is, like so many top ll manipulators, stronger the left than on the right.

A score of England caps behind him. He has ighted crowds all over e world.

Now he is recovered fully m a leg break last season, will be continuing to do for a long time to come.

# HE ONLY TRAINED ON FRIDAYS

**D**ID you ever hear the story of the famous player who, some weeks, didn't even bother to go to the ground for training until the Friday—AND THEN ONLY BECAUSE IT WAS PAY DAY ?

Yes, he had to be very special to get away with this sort of thing. And he certainly was . . .

His name was TOM WARING—though never known as other than "Pongo"—and he played centre-forward for Aston Villa and Barnsley.

Waring's fantastic ability to "screen" the ball, shutting it off from defenders in tantalising and devastating manner, his explosive shooting and heading power—all are still fondly recalled by vintage fans in the Midlands.

So is the day he turned out against Arsenal—with a broken arm in a plaster.

"Pongo" Waring—still living around Birkenhead—is one of the legendary men of football. One whose contribution to the game can never be measured by entries in the record book. However notable may be the feats recorded.

And there are so many more of these football legends . . .

❋

**N**OW coaching takes up as much of the weekly programme of club preparation, the story of the late TOMMY McINALLY claims a place.

This brilliant ball-playing Scottish internationalist of Celtic always believed in having fun with his games.

He was finishing his career with the now defunct Third Lanark—when the trainer decided on a bit of blackboard coaching.

Deep in an illustration of how an attack on goal should be developed, the man at the blackboard was suddenly confronted by "Tommy The Jester"—who let go with a kick that sent the whole show flying.

"What the . . .!" exclaimed the shocked trainer.

"That's a defender stepping in to wreck the move," was the glib explanation from this man who played his football "by ear" only.

**BRYN JONES**

❋

**S**TILL in the inside-forward department we find BRYN JONES—the Welshman whose £14,000 transfer from Wolves to Arsenal was a pre-1939-45 war sensation.

So outstanding was this little man in his day it used to be said the Welsh international selectors always chose "Bryn and ten others."

Certainly their team used to revolve around him. That was made evident when Wales played Scotland one misty, murky day in Dundee.

Wales' stocking colours were red. But, in such

## How Often You See It Reported —"The

I SPY A SPY

PLAYERS · OFFICIALS · SPIES

"HEY REF.!"

"WE CAN'T GO ON MEETING LIKE THIS!"

# BECAUSE THAT WAS PAY DAY

**TOM FINNEY**

conditions of visibility, this danger man was given a pair of bright yellow hose —so he could be more easily pinpointed by his mates.

The plan worked a treat, too. Wales won 2-1 —with the scheming of Jones a vital factor.

❋

FRANCIS LEE is currently penalty king of Manchester City. Before the war, City had another spot-kick expert in ALEC HERD, a Scottish internationalist.

Before coming to Maine Road, Alec played for Hamilton Academicals in the Scottish League. On one remarkable day, he scored for them from three penalty kicks.

As he went to take the first, an opponent, trying to unsettle him, asked Herd where he was to put the ball.

"To the right of the 'keeper," was the reply. And he did just that.

Stepping forward for No. 2, he was again asked where the ball was going. "To the left," said Alec —and stuck the kick neatly past the 'keeper's left hand.

Came the third award. This time the opposition didn't bother to ask. The ball whistled past the 'keeper once more.

As the players went back to the centre circle, an opponent asked Herd why he hadn't nominated his last penalty. Said Herd—"I wasn't asked. Anyway I thought I might give the poor goalie a chance if I didn't make up my mind."

❋

UNLIKE almost every big star of the game, TOM FINNEY played for only one club — Preston North End. Yet he could have become the first £100-a-week British player. He could have received a signing-on fee of £10,000 — for only two years' work.

The offer came to Tom after a successful 1952 European tour with the England team.

From an Italian millionaire — Prince Roberto Lanza di Trabia — it included a free villa on the Mediterranean, a brand new Continental car, and free travel to Italy for Tom's wife and family.

The Prince was president of the Palermo club, in Sicily.

Tom laughs, " It now seems a little hard to believe. The first time I went to Italy I was a private in the British Army . . . glad of the chance to have a game as a break from the sweat of the war. Six years later I was offered a prince's ransom to play the same game."

But Preston would not agree — and Tom did not press for the chance to make a quick fortune.

" I liked Preston, my home and my friends. Sometimes they can be more important than money."

## Had A Man Spying On Opponents-To-Be"

'SAY WHAT YOU LIKE — I THINK THAT LINESMAN'S PASSING MESSAGES!"

"WE'VE GOT WAYS TO MAKE YOU TALK!"

THE request on the big notice-board at Stamford Bridge seems a bit out of line with what is happening on the field—as Chelsea players descend on Peter Houseman (No. 11) with their hugs and back-claps after he'd scored against Wolves. That's Peter's face—inset.

## QUICK SUB

BARRY ENDEAN, Blackburn Rovers, was substituted against Port Vale last season — without even getting on to the pitch!

He broke down with a leg injury while warming up in the dressing-room. The teams had already been declared to the referee. Blackburn were unable to put in a replacement.

So Blackburn officially had to bring in their substitute — before the match started!

### SPOT-OFF

GARSINGTON beat Heading-ton Amateurs 5-0 in an Oxford Intermediate Cup first-round replay. They also missed SIX penalties — against THREE different 'keepers used by their opponents.

## Anti-Bull Rush

F.C. PARDOZ of Argentina once played in brilliant all-red.

Now they've changed to blue and white.

Pardoz are a poor club. They couldn't afford to mend the holes in the fence that separated them from a field . . . where bulls were kept.

## The Birds, The Bees and the Beasts

A MENAGERIE, with an aviary on the side — that's this line-up of nicknames given to English League clubs —

**BLUEBIRDS** — Barrow and Cardiff.

**BEES** — Brentford.

**ROBINS** — Bristol City, Swindon and Wrexham.

**RAMS** — Derby County.

**TERRIERS** — Huddersfield Town.

**TIGERS** — Hull City.

**STAGS** — Mansfield Town.

**LIONS** — Millwall.

**MAGPIES** — Newcastle United and Notts County.

**CANARIES** — Norwich.

**OWLS** — Sheffield Wed.

**SWANS** — Swansea.

**GULLS** — Torquay.

**HORNETS** — Watford.

**WOLVES** — Wolverhampton.

BIRMINGHAM CITY decided every time one of their players hit a hat-trick they'd present him with the match ball.

Centre-forward Bob Latchford started well — with two three-goal shows inside three weeks.

Above, you see him showing-off his awards — with manager Freddie Goodwin.

## • Here — and Gone

WHO holds the record for shortest spell with one club?

It's a fair bet the distinction belongs to Alan Hellyer. His career with Southern League Bath City lasted just five hours.

After he had signed, Alan found he would be unable to get time off work for the club's mid-week games.

The contract was ripped up by mutual agreement.

## • Rule of Ten

VENEZUELA have decided to reduce the number of foreign players allowed per team to — TEN.

At last count 90 per cent. of the country's professionals were born abroad.

Do you wonder the Venezuelan national team doesn't figure too prominently in the world scene.

### Start of Something Big

FIRST-EVER penalty kick was taken in the Airdrie v. Royal Albert Airdrie Charity Cup final on June 6, 1891.

It was just four days after the International Board meeting in Glasgow had passed the law authorising the award.

Fifteen minutes after the start, Royal Albert were awarded a spot-kick. James McCluggage scored.

## The Team With A Sty In Its Eye

CHRIS CHEVERTON of Waterlooville — the Southern League club — is a highly-superstitious fellow.

When he spent the season before last without ever playing in a losing side — Chris reckoned some sort of special fortune-bringer must be on his side.

Suddenly it came to him — HE HAD ALWAYS SEEN A PIG ON HIS WAY TO A MATCH.

Chris told his team-mates about it . . .

His superstitions were so respected that, nowadays, Waterlooville feel apprehensive about the outcome of a game if they don't come across some sort of porker on their way to the ground.

# FOOTBALL

## Come Trancing

NEW BRIGHTON (Cheshire League) had conceded 40 goals, lost eight games on the trot, were second-bottom of the table. So a professional hypnotist was called in.

As the players relaxed in the dressing-room just before the kick-off and during the interval, they were put in a light trance.

At half-time, New Brighton were leading Hyde United 3-0. Final result — 3-3.

## BIRD'S-EYE VIEW

THE roof of one of Stockport County's stands sprang a few leaks.

When repairs were made, advertisements were introduced up there.

No spectator can see them — but County's ground lies directly under the flight path to Manchester Airport.

The adverts can be seen clearly by the aircraft passengers.

## JACK'S AN ACE

JACK DAVIES, skipper of Todmorden (Halifax and District League), took to the stocks in a club fund-raising effort.

He was bombarded with wet sponges, buckets of water, tomatoes, yoghourt and eggs for over an hour.

But he reckoned it all worthwhile. His efforts raised £6.

## REVENGE !

FANS of Mexican club El Cuervo were riled when their team was beaten 4-3 by El Deslizadero.

Two of them decided to lie in wait for the man who scored the winner—Alberto Santiago.

As he was boarding the team bus outside the ground, they shot him four times.

Alberto was rushed to hospital—but was dead on arrival.

### BLUNDER IN ICELAND

WHEN a Bahamas touring team went to Iceland, each player was presented with raincoat, sou'wester and a pair of galoshes after a match with a team from a Reykjavik rubber factory.

Diplomatically, nobody mentioned it rains in the Bahamas, on average, on only two days a year.

## A Truly Great Grandad

EMBLETON F.C. (Northumberland) were a man short. Spectator Les Turnbull, there to watch two of his sons play, volunteered to stand in.

He borrowed jersey, boots that were two sizes too big for him, and tucked his trousers into his socks.

Les cracked in two goals to help Embleton beat Long Horsley 4-1.

And all the time his wife, also there, was begging him to pack up.

For Les was a 53-year-old grandad !

### OUT IN SPOTS

FULL time was reached in the Mexican Cup final between Leon and Zacatepeo without a goal being scored.

Still no goal in extra time — so it was decided to settle with penalty-kicks.

Forty had to be taken before Leon ran out winners by 10-9. Of the other spot-kicks 16 were saved and five sent wide.

## "Mr Bowler Hat"

THIS was the very personal crest on the card sent to friends last Christmas by Mr Jimmy Brownlie, 87-year-old former Third Lanark and Scotland goalkeeper.

Mr Brownlie always wears a bowler hat on match days, always smokes a pipe — and wouldn't let a Saturday go by without having a go on the football coupons.

So the friend who made up the crest had plenty to work on . . .

## • Emergency Man

IT'S a toss-up whether Dubliner Shaun O'Keefe will return home after watching a football match — or whether he'll end up in hospital.

Seven times has Shaun been rushed from a football ground to a special care unit—each time suffering a heart attack.

## • Ski-Man Scorer

CHAMPIONS of Norway last season were Rosenberg Trondheim — formerly managed by Englishman George Curtis.

Top scorer was winger Wirkola, an Olympic Gold Medallist — at ski jumping!

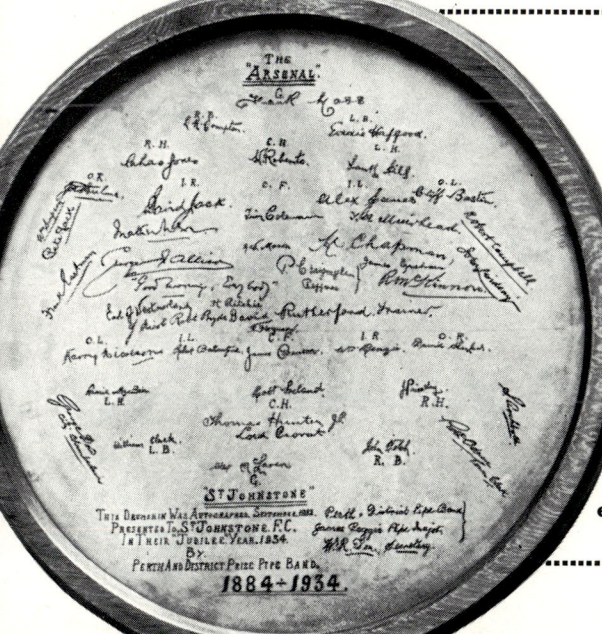

# Sign on the Drum, Chum

MATCH mementoes come in all sizes, shapes — and forms.

Here is a picture of an autographed drumskin — presented to Scottish First Division club St Johnstone by the band which played at their show game with Arsenal in 1932.

Famous names of the past are inscribed all over it.

Highbury notables like Frank Moss, Leslie Compton, Eddie Hapgood, Frank Hill, Joe Hulme, David Jack, Alec James and Cliff Bastin.

St Johnstone stalwarts in Sandy McLaren, Johnny Welsh, Laurie MacBain and Harry Nicholson.

That showman among managers, George Allison of Arsenal, had added his radio greeting, " Good morning, everybody."

And there was even a belted Earl in the party.

**MIKE SUMMERBEE, Manchester City**

PAUL FLETCHER, Burnley

# MY BOY, ALAN

### By— HIS DAD
(Manager Alan Ball of Preston North End)

I WAS in the army on National Service, serving my stint in Germany, when I got word my wife had given birth to a baby boy.

Within minutes I had decided to help make him a great footballer. I didn't think of anything else for him ever again.

When I got home and saw his little red head, I knew immediately what I wanted him to be — a perpetual motion player. A red bobbing head constantly moving. And everybody seeing him moving *all the time* because of that red hair.

I want to tell you about the making of my son as a great footballer. To tell you about his formative football childhood. The plans, the sweat, the dreams, the coaching, the rows . . . everything that made my boy the greatest inside-right in Europe today.

Fifty-seven times capped for England, winner of a World Cup-winners' medal, League Championship medal, two F.A. Cup runners-up medals and the first player in Britain to be transferred for £220,000.

## PRESENTS ARE VETTED

I KNEW he would make it right to the very top. And so did the rest of the family. Alan's uncles, aunts, grandads and grandmums all got the message from me right at the start.

I vetted all of the Christmas and birthday presents Alan got from his first birthday on.

I would get in touch with them all to make sure his presents were something to do with sport. I wanted to be sure all his energies and interests went into physical sport.

His first pair of football boots were there and waiting for him to walk. The second he could walk — when he was two — I put him in full football strip and football boots.

We went out into the back garden and for an hour I patiently rolled a football at him. He started to poke it back to me. He loved the little game we were playing.

This ritual we did almost every day until he was five years old. He "lived" football from the beginning.

At that time I was manager of a non-league side — Oswestry Town. Alan travelled with us everywhere. Trained with us. Changed with us. Got into the big bath with all of us.

And I continued to punish him hard in our own little personal training sessions.

He had a terrible habit of closing his eyes

86

**ALAN BALL, Senior**

also outlast the others, is bound to come out on the very top.

When he was five years old I had the doctor check on his physical well-being. I knew then he would respond to anything I asked him to do in training. Even though he was so skinny and weak-looking.

The doc had told me—" Young Alan has a big, strong heart, good lungs and is a perfect little boy."

This, coupled to the enormous amount of training I put him through, plus his competitive instinct, made him a great all-round sportsman.

He swam for his county; still holds the record for a mile run by a 14-year-old in Lancashire; at 17 years of age he scored 212 for Kersley in the Bolton Cricket League; and at 15 finished 17th out of over 200 cross-country runners in an under-18 race.

These most certainly were the days that made Alan into the star player he is now.

And yet few people really wanted him at the start. I had to trick Ron Suart—then manager of Blackpool—into watching him in a trial.

## SIGNED BY BLACKPOOL

When he left school I asked Alan what he wanted to do. " Be a professional footballer," he answered.

That was my intention, too. So I told him not to work. I gave him training schedules and left him at home.

He went down to Wolves for a trial. But they said he was too small.

Then he went to Bolton. He became an apprentice there, but nobody seemed to think he would make the grade.

So, one day, I went down to see Ron Suart. I told him I had seen a very promising kid called Alan James.

Alan's full name is Alan James Ball. So I wasn't telling much of a lie, was I?

He went along to Squires Gate to play in a practice match with the Blackpool players. At half-time Ron Suart pulled him out of the game and asked him to sign for Blackpool.

We asked Bolton. They did not want him—and he had started his career.

That, basically, is the story of how I made my son Alan into a world-class footballer.

What has happened to him since he turned 16 came about because of those tough, formative years.

Of course, his love for the game knew no bounds. For instance . . .

He was just a kid when we went to Spain on holiday. First morning there I noticed a team sheet pinned to the wall in the dining-room.

It was a team selected by Alan from our hotel to play a team from a neighbouring hotel.

He organised that. During the fortnight's holiday we played six other hotels.

Some boy . . .

when he headed a ball. So I kept him at heading for two hours solid.

He never complained. Just kept on heading the ball and heading it and heading it. He would never be beaten.

Once I remember him heading that ball until his forehead was bleeding slightly. But he did not complain. He wanted to succeed. To improve.

We must have spent 100 hours on this heading problem. His forehead became hardened. He doesn't close his eyes when he heads the ball now!

His mum was not all that pleased. She was upset when he came home with that blood on his forehead. I told her she should look after our daughter and I would look after our son. A boy for you, a girl for me.

I must make it clear Alan never once complained or indicated that he did not want to become a footballer.

Not even when I taught him that, out on a football field, life was tough. He would get his legs rapped hard and there would be a lot of pain.

*I taught him this by repeatedly kicking him on the shins.*

That is how he learned to stand up to everything in the tough midfield areas.

But, deep down, as I said, I wanted him to be a perpetual motion man. After all, running is a vital part of the game.

Any player who first of all has the skills, and can

# MEN OF LIVERPOOL

**Steve Heighway**

**Chris Lawler**

The story of a big break-through, by . . .
**ALEC LINDSAY**
Liverpool

# HAUNTED
## —By My £60,000 Transfer Fee

**P**ERSONAL attitude, confidence, a feeling of being at home . . . these are some of the unseen elements that can make or break a footballer.

They certainly had a bearing on my slow progress at Anfield under the great Bill Shankly — and alongside some of the finest players in Britain.

You see, when I went to Liverpool from Bury for £60,000 almost three years ago, I lacked those three vital ingredients for success.

To me that was an enormous fee. It more or less haunted me for the first 18 months.

Could I justify it? Was I good enough? What did players like Peter Thompson, Tommy Smith, Ian St John think of me?

Some players seem to be able to carry a big price label and not worry. Not me! And it showed.

I felt far from at home in that Liverpool dressing-room. I suppose part of the trouble is that my interests are so different from most players these days.

I love to go shooting. Or to take the ferrets out and get rabbits. Then sometimes I go fishing. I have caught foxes.

As a kid I was up every morning at dawn and out exercising my brother's greyhounds. We lived on the

**ALEC LINDSAY**
*—stylist among kickers*

G

# AN AMAZING TRANSFORMATION

outskirts of Bury, and I would walk for miles and miles with the greyhounds.

I would get back home in time for my paper round before going to school.

After school I would deliver the evening papers and then take the greyhounds out again.

Back home for tea and out again to play football —or go after hares or rabbits or fishing.

Yes, I'm a country boy at heart. Not for me the night clubs, discotheques, boutiques and business interests.

Of course, now I can indulge myself at my outdoor hobby. I can afford good guns to go shooting.

Occasionally I get invitations to go out after grouse and pheasants. That is wonderful. So is my career now with the great Liverpool. But it was tough making the grade.

At Bury I had been basically an attacking wing half. I liked to come through from deep positions. So my first selection at Liverpool was in a number 8 shirt. I didn't score and was dropped. Not much of a start, was it?

I was out of the first team for four months, then got two games with a number 10 on my back. Dropped and back again at left back . . . then dropped.

That was it for the 69-70 season. I had been bought for what I thought was a staggering fee and managed to get into the first team only four times.

" Ach, I never wanted to be picked for the international team, anyway."

When I started the following season still out of the first team — and in the reserves as a striker — I honestly began to think the boss was thinking he had bought a duck egg.

But, after missing the first six games and becoming really worried, I saw my name on the team sheet at left-back to play Newcastle at St James's Park.

I knew it was a test. I HAD to do it. And I did. I played well. I never looked back. I was injured a couple of times, but basically I felt I had made the grade.

Last season I missed only a handful of games. My confidence is now top-line. I have forgotten about the fee. I AM A LIVERPOOL PLAYER! I fear nobody.

I suppose that, as a team, Liverpool went through the same sort of experience as me last season.

We started unsure of ourselves. The way I had begun at Anfield. We were a new team, with the experience of the cup final behind us. We were hopeful. And, needless to say, the boss was adamant this would be our season.

But the results were up and down. At one point,

three months from the end of the programme, we were seventh from the top of the table.

AND ALL THE TIME THE BOSS WAS INSISTING WE WOULD WIN THE CHAMPION-SHIP! He just would not accept we weren't good enough. And we nearly made it . . .

We were knocked out of the F.A. Cup by Leeds. The season looked over. Out of Europe, out of the League Cup, out of the cup and seventh in the table.

We had talks. Well, maybe I should say Mr Shankly held some high-pressure psychology courses. Him talking and us listening.

For practically a whole week he told us we now had to go on and win every game and take the title. You just cannot knock this Scotsman down.

Well, we went out and won ELEVEN OF OUR NEXT TWELVE GAMES. We drew the other one. We scored 29 goals in that run and conceded 2.

What a transformation!

But the boss took it as though it were just to be expected. Then came the last two games of the season — away to Derby and Arsenal.

Derby was probably the worse in terms of nerves. We lost our composure and Derby won 1-0.

But we still had a chance . . . if we could beat Arsenal at Highbury. Emlyn Hughes hit the woodwork and John Toshack scored, but it was judged offside. No goals were scored that night. So we lost a championship we never expected to challenge for.

That was a desperate disappointment. But I can look back on last season and at least claim I established myself.

From my early days I aimed at becoming a professional footballer. I played for the Bury Town Boys' team, and when I was 14 Bury asked me along to train with them.

After a couple of nights I was cheesed off and packed up going to Gigg Lane. But when time came to leave school, at 15, I only knew I was going to be a professional footballer.

Mr Talbot, who ran the boys' team, phoned Bury and told them if they did not sign me they would lose out on a great player.

They took me on. I got £5 a week and had a lot of fun. Until Liverpool signed me and I started to worry.

Last season may have marked my break-through at Anfield. It also was the first season I ever fell foul of referees. I was booked three times.

That was a blow. And when I was fined £100 I was furious. Not at any injustice—just at the fact I had thrown away a hundred quid.

# MAN WITH TWO FACES

The face at the top of this page is the face of JOHN HOLLINS of Chelsea. The player putting his all into a shot at goal is also Hollins.

How appearances change when action and effort is called for—and the pressure's on, too!

The fellow making a vain attempt to baulk Hollins is PAUL HARRIS, Orient.

DAVID ALLISON — ex-Blackpool colt. Father (below) is MALCOLM ALLISON, Manchester City manager.

KEVIN BOND — with Bournemouth, managed by his father, JOHN BOND — seen watching his young hopeful at shooting practice.

# IT'S
# THE BI

Noted football fathe
are looking all set to
in the ga

RUSSELL ALLEN, West Bromwich Albion, is son of RONNIE ALLEN, far-travelled manager (right).

LAWREN
ward LAV

STEPHEN WADDINGTON,
Stoke City, with his dad,
City's manager.

OD

sons who
a splash

MICHAEL DOCHERTY,
Burnley, and the "old
man," Scotland team
manager Tommy ("The
Doc").

JIMMY CASKIE,
Clydebank, is an
outside-left—as was
his father, Jimmy—
ex - St Johnstone,
Everton and Ran-
gers.

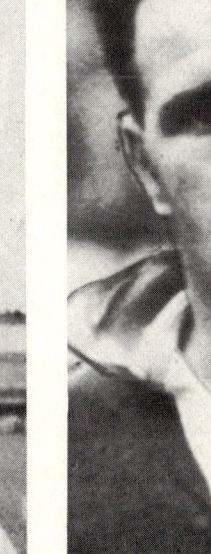

16-year-old son of ex-Hibs and Scotland centre-for-
ball of different shape. He is a member of Edin-
gh's Melville College rugby team.

BETWEEN Arsenal's Highbury stadium and Brentford's Griffin Park there are fifteen miles — and a world of difference in football standards.

The difference between a top London club and a Cinderella outfit.

Last season Brentford were the "odd bods" of London's eleven clubs.

Five were in the First Division, five in the Second — with "The Bees" tucked away in League Four.

Yet they are probably the most remarkable of all the London clubs.

Their story tells of relegation from the First Division in season 1946-47 — the first after the 1939-45 war — and a "drift" that finally ended in Division Four, followed by a fight against take-over bids. And, now, they have set foot on the ladder again with promotion to the Third Division.

For the past five years they have run on a shoe-string budget — sometimes with a playing staff only 12 strong. At one time they were saddled with a debt of £104,000.

This season workmen took away a "financial barometer" from outside the Brentford ground. It showed how the club was going about clearing its £104,000 debt. That has now been wiped out.

At their blackest cash period "The Bees" came near to being taken over by Queen's Park Rangers. The idea was Q.P.R. should sell their Loftus Road ground and take over the 40,000 - capacity Griffin Park set-up of their neighbours.

Brentford decided to fight on. They'd run just one team, keep clear of transfer deals, go about squaring debts and start again.

"We cut everything to the bone," says general manager Dennis Piggott. "And extra money was

**FRANK BLUNSTONE —**
*man of all trades*

produced by running special schemes. We have survived. Now we are beginning to see daylight."

Comparison with Arsenal is the best way to pinpoint just how hard it has been for Brentford to get themselves in position to challenge the bigger London teams.

When Arsenal won the League-F.A. Cup double, they paid £245,418 in wages. Brentford's wage bill for that season was £40,470 — less than three Arsenal first-team players collected between them.

Arsenal spent £43,083 in travel, training, hotels. Brentford's bill was £4000 — one tenth of the Arsenal figure.

While the Gunners were travelling first class and staying at the top hotels, "The Bees" were making long-distance coach trips to places like Hartlepool and Workington. Coming back overnight to avoid accommodation costs.

Arsenal have a manager, first team coach, reserve team coach, youth team coach, chief scout, district scouts — and a whole host

★

*JOHN O'MARA — the "unknown" now worth eighty times his buying price*

★

of other helpers behind the scenes.

During their stickiest times, Brentford had a staff of manager Frank Blunstone, coach Frank Blunstone, chief scout Frank Blunstone, kit man Frank Blunstone, and, during the summer, painter-in-chief Frank Blunstone.

This, then, is the route by which Brentford have managed to make a profit over these past five years. It's some achievement, considering not more than a dozen of the 92 Football League clubs seem able to end a season out of the red.

The club has also made shrewd buys. Like the £750 paid to Southern League Wimbledon for an unknown centre-forward named John O'Mara. He was rated a £60,000 man last season.

They also paid West Ham United £12,000 for striker Roger Cross — then sold him to Fulham for £30,000.

This season Brentford expect bigger things.

Their main competition comes from other West London clubs like Chelsea, Queen's Park Rangers and Fulham.

But they were a First Division team before such as Q.P.R. and Fulham had their spells at the top — and while West Ham United were a Second Division side.

"Our system is the only one by which a small club can survive," says Frank Blunstone. "But we don't mean to be small much longer."

# THEY WERE ONCE HIS CLUB MATES....

Alan Gilzean
Spurs.

Martin Buchan
Manchester United

Jim Steele
Southampton

Charlie Cooke
Chelsea.

# OLD PALS GALLERY

**W**HEN Dundee offered me a fortnight's trial as a 17-year-old in 1963, it came right out of the blue.

Why — I didn't even own a decent pair of football boots for the job.

I'd played for the first eleven at school in Dumbarton along with John O'Hare (Derby) and Evan Williams (Celtic), but was planning to go to university the following year and forget football.

Indeed, if I hadn't failed my Higher English I would already have been preparing to start university and turned my nose up at Dundee's offer. Instead, I was just lazing around during the summer break before going back to school to repeat my English.

I really had no intention of signing for Dundee — although I did buy myself new boots on the way to Dens Park.

The only suitably-sized pair in the shop were pure white. So, I suppose, I could lay claim to

*Drawn by*
**STEVE MURRAY**
The Aberdeen team captain who also writes about . . .
**"MY DOUBLE TARGET"**

**STEVE MURRAY**

wearing these novel type before Alan Ball and Co. came along to make them universally popular.

At the end of my trial spell I was getting ready to go home when the Dundee manager, Bob Shankly, asked me to stay over for one final game — a public trial.

In those days Scottish clubs usually played eve-of-season games consisting of first-team against the reserves.

There I was, just a raw laddie in white boots, chasing and harrying against some of Scotland's best-known players. Alec. Hamilton, Ian Ure, Gordon Smith and Alan Gilzean among them.

So you can imagine my complete surprise when, after the game, Mr Shankly offered to sign me.

Remember — Dundee were a side right on top at that time, having reached the semi-final of the European Cup the previous season.

I reckon I was so surprised I signed immediately — forgetting all about my university ideas.

I was so green behind the ears I didn't even know I was

# I HAD TO SAY "NO" TO TOMMY DOCHERTY

entitled to the £20 signing-on fee which was handed to me.

Still, although my turning professional was done on impulse, it's something I've never regretted.

After all, I've since played for Scotland at Under-23, League and full international level. Played in the European Cup-Winners' Cup, Fairs' Cup and U.E.F.A. Cup. And, following a run as captain of Dundee, I am now skippering my second senior club, Aberdeen.

But I haven't let all that completely cloud my schoolboy ambition of university. I've found a way, by taking the Open University course in mathematics and science, hoping for an honours degree in both.

At one time I thought of part-time football and university on a full-time basis. I'm glad I didn't, the way things are working out now. Although it means life is really hectic. There's never a minute to spare.

But I'm convinced it will all be worth while in the end. You see, when I finish playing football, I've no thoughts about staying in the game as a coach or manager. I want to lecture at university.

This Open University is a wonderful set-up. It's practically all done from television lectures. Sort of like a live correspondence course. It also means I'm often up until the early hours of the morning trying to work out, say, a chemistry experiment.

Fortunately, it doesn't interfere with my football in the slightest.

The only thing I've had to sacrifice is one Scottish League cap. In March of last season the Scotland team manager, Tommy Docherty, wanted me to play in the inter-League game against England at Middlesbrough.

But he was most understanding when I asked to be left out because I had exams later that month.

As it is, I seem to thrive on the extra work. I've just completed my most successful season, although I haven't actually won a football honour apart from my caps and a Drybrough Cup-winner's medal.

The year I was transferred to Aberdeen for £50,000 they won the Scottish Cup—beating Celtic 3-1 in the final. But I had to watch from the stand at Hampden. I was already cup-tied for Dundee that season.

Strange thing was, Aberdeen had actually made an offer for me before the Cup started. But Dundee wanted to keep me until they were knocked out of the competition. The Dens Parkers themselves got to the semi-final before losing to Celtic 2-1. But I was injured and missed that game.

You can see, then, why I'm desperate to help Aberdeen win something.

In my early days with Dundee they, too, reached the Scottish Cup Final. But I hadn't made the first team then.

It was in those early days as a reserve I gained my Higher English to add to the Higher passes in maths and science I'd taken at school. That finally gave me university qualifications.

And much of it was to the credit of the then Dundee second team coach and former player, Gerry Follon. As a full-time school teacher, Gerry only came to Dens in the evenings. But he helped me so much to pass the English exam.

But don't think, because of my studies, I'm not ambitious. I wouldn't mind a crack at English football. You see, the great thing about this Open University is you can do the course anywhere. As long as you have " telly."

In my time I've been team-mates with four players who have broken the Scottish record transfer fee.

## SECRET BEHIND ALL MY ENERGY

Just after I joined Dundee, Ian Ure went on " strike." He refused terms for the new season and was determined to play in England. Eventually Arsenal paid £67,000, an all-time Scottish high at that time.

Then there was Alan Gilzean. He moved on to Spurs for £72,500 — thereby increasing the record. Charlie Cooke soon followed for just over that figure to Chelsea.

Just before I left Dundee for Pittodrie another bright youngster in Jim Steele burst on to the scene. He, of course, joined Southampton for £70,000.

Then last season Aberdeen transferred Martin Buchan to Manchester United for £130,000. The present Scottish record fee.

I get around a lot during a game. So people often ask me where I get all my energy from.

I'm fortunate in never having to diet. So probably the answer is the wonderful cooking of my wife, Cathy, a school teacher. I eat everything she puts down for me. This, along with Aberdeen's commando-style training, keeps me fit as anyone in the game.

Although I play midfield, I finished up Aberdeen's second-top goal-scorer last season. I suppose I must be what you'd call an undisciplined anchor man.

My great get-away from it all, football and studies, is to sit down and sketch. Usually character sketches.

Until recently I wrote a monthly article for the church magazine, complete with my own illustrations. A couple of times I've done sketches for newspapers before a big game, giving my light-hearted side to it.

At one time I actually thought of going to art college.

My other great relaxation is having at least a three-week holiday abroad every summer. Spent usually lying on a beach absorbing all the sun I can get.

I then come back feeling refreshed, ready for another year of football and studies.

**ERIC MARTIN**, Southampton

## GLASGOW...NORWICH...BRAZIL.

**They may be a long way apart, but they add up – to a fantastic season for me.**

In GLASGOW I won a Scottish League Cup winners' medal with just-promoted Partick Thistle. Leading 4-0 at half-time in the final against Celtic, and eventually winning 4-1, Thistle were the only side in Europe that really slammed the Scottish champions last season.

In NORWICH, having joined City, I became one of a Second Division Championship team for the second season running. Going with Norwich into Division One for the first time in their history.

And so to BRAZIL — where I was a member of the Scotland squad for the " Mini World Cup."

Quite a sequence . . .

Of course, the " big one " was Norwich making the First Division.

I joined Norwich just before the transfer deadline, played in 13 matches, scored four goals — and by the end of it all had played some part in taking the club into the First Division.

But how I wondered after my first game!

The move from Partick Thistle had been a swift one. Suddenly I found myself as the fellow Norwich seemed to be banking on to clinch their promotion effort.

My first appearance was at St Andrew's against Birmingham City — the side right up with Norwich in the promotion stakes. The side that eventually went along with us into Division One.

We were beaten a shattering 4-0.

I needn't have worried. My next match was against Sunderland at Carrow Road. The TV cameras came along and I had the kind of home debut every player dreams about.

I scored the goal that won a vital point, was spotlighted on TV and

## 'After a shattering start —I had the kind of home debut every player dreams about'

got dozens of letters from the fans welcoming me to Norwich.

I felt I had really arrived.

" A forward cast in the old mould. Tough, fearless, no slouch in football skills, and with an unquenchable thirst for goals. A crowd-pleasing personality," said one newspaper report.

There was temptation to cut it out and send it to the five clubs that had turned me down early in my career — Stirling Albion, Hibs, Airdrie, Liverpool and Forfar Athletic.

Mostly their reaction was on the lines of, " Sorry, son, but you'll need to fill out a bit before we can use you."

I suppose the point was valid. I was 5 ft. 7 in. and 10 stone then. Now I'm 5 ft. 10½ in. and 12 stone.

It's marvellous the difference a few inches and a few pounds can make to a striker.

The only club out of the five I did not give a real chance to was Liverpool — who *did* take me on trial.

But I was a 17-year-old from just outside of Stirling then. I was terribly homesick in Liverpool, and didn't stay long enough to give the club a real chance to assess the growing possibilities of the very young Jim Bone.

When I was transferred from Partick Thistle to Norwich I was 22. And I think a lot of folk felt the pressures of stepping into a side running for promotion would affect

my game. Particularly after that first match against Birmingham City.

But I found the pressures lifted me. Perhaps I was in the right shape to accept them — having helped Thistle win promotion from the Scottish Second Division and gone through that high pressure Hampden show that finished so sensationally.

Anyhow, it was great to get back into an exciting promotion atmosphere — and the promise of even greater things to come.

I thought it would be tough moving to England . . .

In Scotland I'd been a part-timer. During the day I worked as a Coal Board electrician — underground most of the time. I kept fit by training a couple of evenings a week.

During the miners' strike, I played for the Scottish Under-23's against England at Derby. I enjoyed taking part in a game without the worry of getting back to work next morning.

In England I found I had to work a lot more off the ball. Running a lot farther — and a lot harder.

I also thought I'd wear away to a shadow with full-time training. Instead, after losing a couple of pounds at the start, I started putting on weight. At the end of the season I was four pounds heavier than when a part-timer.

My short spell at Norwich last

# JIMMY BONE

season convinced me we are to have the crowd behind us.

We clinched the title in two away matches with Orient and Watford. And enough fans came with us to make every player appreciate what Carrow Road support can mean.

Up to this moment of going into the First Division, I thought nothing could have topped the Partick Thistle win over Celtic at Hampden Park earlier in the season.

That was the biggest moment in my five seasons with Partick, whom I joined from the junior club Airth Castle Rovers.

I think I'll really settle in East Anglia. There's a great atmosphere about the place. And, from the word go, everybody made me feel at home.

One of the first players I met was Duncan Forbes, a dark-haired Scot from Edinburgh. He was the club skipper, but had been out of action for five months due to injury.

"We'll just about start at the same time," said Duncan. "I've been training almost night and day to get back into the side for the final push. It's Division One or bust."

Well, Duncan missed out on my first match against Birmingham City, but was back for the next one against Sunderland. We both stayed in the team until the championship was won.

# ... THE MAN WHO PUT THE BITE INTO NORWICH CITY

# 'GUNNERS' UNDER STRESS

IT'S Leeds United v. Arsenal — last season's F.A. Cup finalists — in their league game at Elland Road. Above — PETER LORIMER gets away with the ball after a despairing tackle by JOHN ROBERTS. Below — FRANK McLINTOCK cuts out a pass intended for ALLAN CLARKE.

# A GOAL TO REMEMBER ....

*I*t wasn't much of a season last time round for Everton. Alan Ball was transferred. Manager Harry Catterick took seriously ill. Results fell away below standard expected of such a club.

But, in almost every gloomy picture, there's a touch of sunlight.

Everton's was the real emergence of PETER SCOTT.

This local 19-year-old, groomed through Everton's junior sides, alternated between the No. 2 and No. 6 jerseys. But, from the start, he looked anything but a newcomer.

Possibly the abiding memory of him for all who saw it was his 37-second goal in the Cup replay against Crystal Palace.

The ball broke to Peter on the edge of the box. He ran on to smash it with such power, it's more than slightly doubtful if goalkeeper John Jackson even saw the shot.

I doubt if goals will be the key factor in Peter's career—his tally was precisely two last season—but his tackling power, speed off the mark and over the distance are likely to bring him a few.

Which will be a bonus on top of his other talents, likely to be used in defence or midfield for his club.

# YOU'LL FIND THEM

**RAY GRAYDON**
(Aston Villa)

**JOHN SISSONS**
(Sheffield Wednesday)

**TOM HUTCHISON**
(Blackpool)

**NICK JENNINGS**
(Portsmouth)

**GORDON TAYLOR**
(Birmingham City)

**R. REES**
(Swansea City)

**KEN FOGGO**
(Norwich City)

**PHIL BOYER**
(Bournemouth)

**GORDON HINDSON**
(Luton Town)

# OUT ON THE WING

**DOUG ALLDER**
(Millwall)

**IAN BUTLER**
(Hull City)

**LES BARRETT**
(Fulham)

**LEIGHTON JAMES**
(Burnley)

**IAN MOIR**
(Shrewsbury Town)

**JIMMY MULLEN**
(Rotherham)

**KEITH PEACOCK**
(Charlton Athletic)

**DON ROGERS**
(Swindon Town)

**DENNIS TUEART**
(Sunderland)

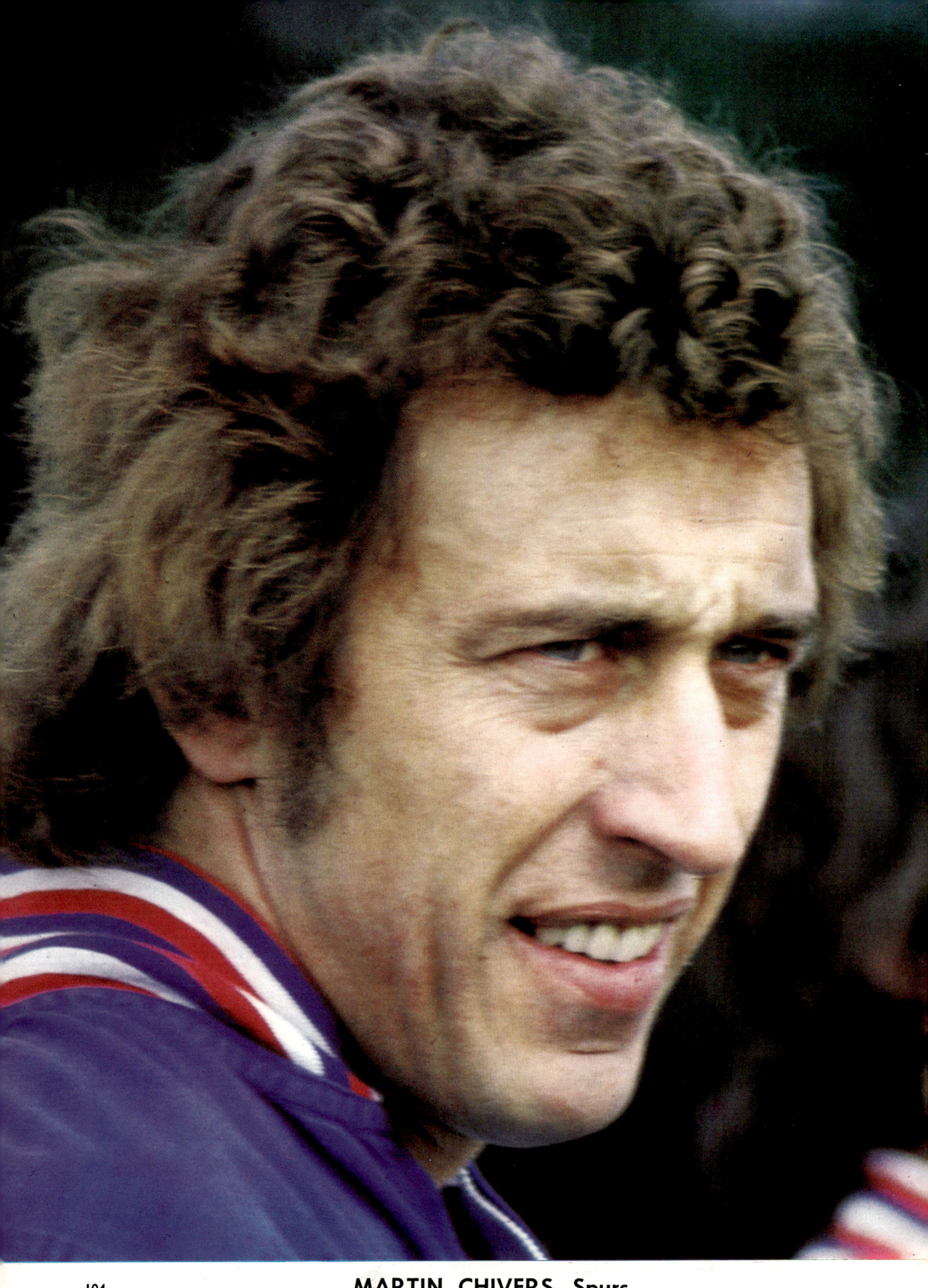

MARTIN CHIVERS, Spurs

**ALAN SUDDICK, Blackpool**

**T**HE best referee, it's always reckoned, is the man who is "never seen."

His control is smooth and efficient. Always in command, he seems to have every player's respect.

His whistle is used most judiciously. His interventions are accepted by both those on field and by super-critical fans on the terracings.

But, sometimes, nature of play doesn't allow a whistler to remain unobtrusive.

He finds himself forced into prominence as the match becomes sour — or too physical — and players grow niggly or over-aggressive, and all sorts of action requires to be taken.

# MEN WHO *WHISTLE* WHILE THEY WORK

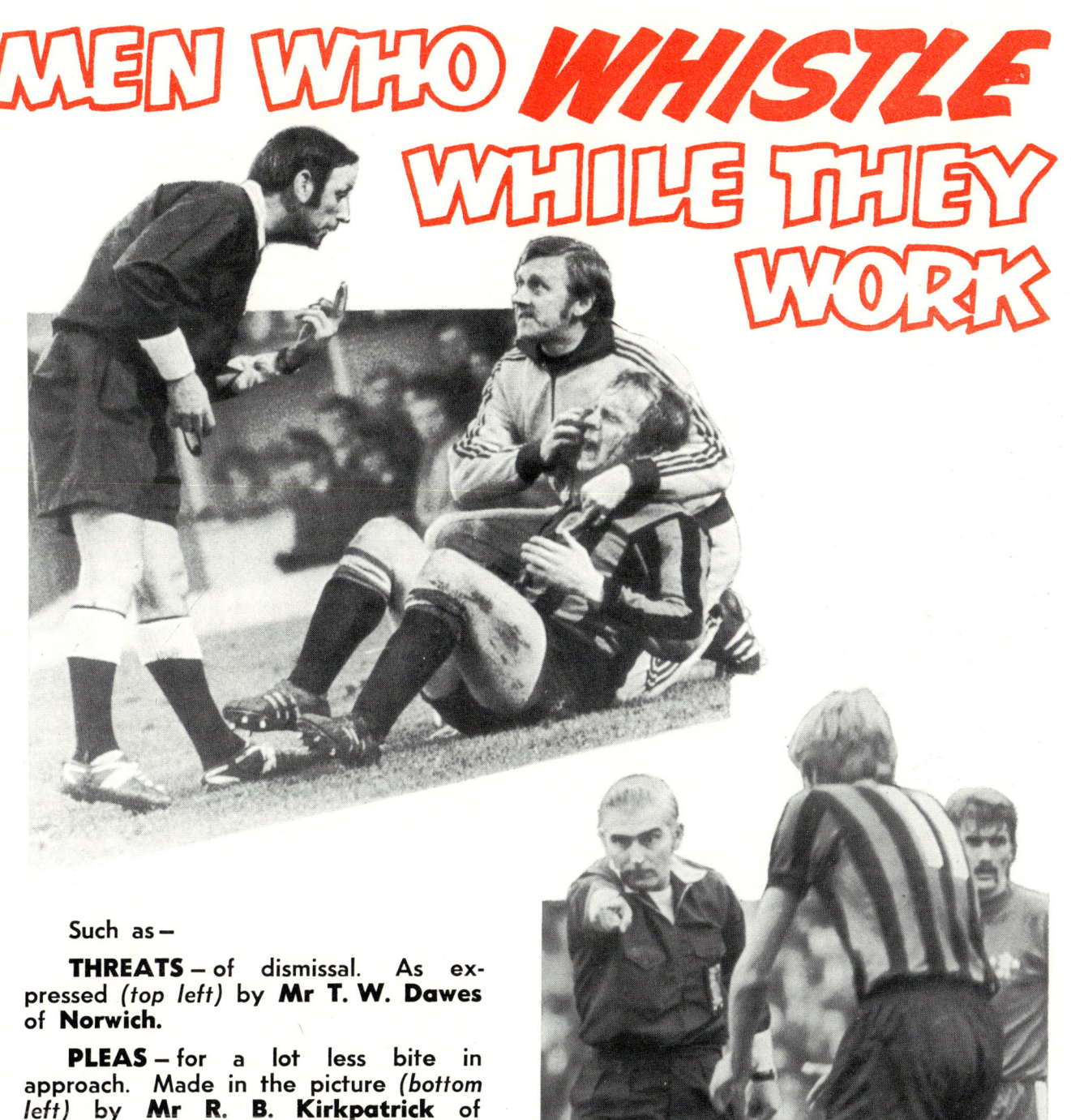

Such as—

**THREATS**—of dismissal. As expressed *(top left)* by **Mr T. W. Dawes** of **Norwich**.

**PLEAS**—for a lot less bite in approach. Made in the picture *(bottom left)* by **Mr R. B. Kirkpatrick** of **Leicester**. And obviously accepted by **Denis Law, Manchester United**.

**ADMONITIONS**—even to a player having attention from the trainer *(top right)*. He is **Francis Lee, Manchester City**—administered to by **Peter Blakey**. The ref—**Mr W. B. Johnson** of **Kendal**.

**PENALTIES**—and **Mr E. D. Wallace** of **Swindon** seems to have no doubt about this one *(bottom right)*. In the picture again is Francis Lee (No. 10)— who has come off second best in a challenge for the ball.

# Red, white and blue—

TRAINING time for Sir Alf Ramsey's squad means variety in colour schemes—as our camerman discovered when he joined the party.

You'll have recognised most of these England men—(1) Team-Manager SIR ALF RAMSEY (2) An earth-bound exercise in which are included TOMMY SMITH, MARTIN PETERS, RALPH COATES, ROY McFARLAND and EMLYN HUGHES. (3) Same set-up—from a different

# at England's H.Q.

ewpoint. (4) ROY McFARLAND adds a new nade to proceedings. (5) An autograph-hunter nd FRANCIS LEE. (6) In his training No. 1's— ODNEY MARSH. (7) Shooting practice—by ALPH COATES. (8) COLIN BELL—with a corner flag that needed replacing. (9) Physical jerks session—featuring (left to right) PETER STOREY, ROY McFARLAND, MARTIN CHIVERS. (10) The World Cup war-horse watches from the sidelines—GEOFF HURST.

## NOVEMBER 3, 1971

AT lunchtime after training with my West Brom mates Manager Don Howe tells me Leeds United want to sign me — and that terms have been agreed.

I feel on top of the world. I immediately buy a Parker fountain pen to sign the forms.

The fee is £170,000.

On the way up the motorway to a roadside motel rendezvous I never stop talking. I couldn't help myself. I was so elated.

Within 10 minutes of meeting Manager Don Revie I sign for Leeds. I still have a medical to pass.

I train at West Brom. There is a barrage of Press men and TV cameras to face. In the evening I drive up to Leeds and check into the hotel my new club has booked for me.

## NOVEMBER 5

ON this Friday morning I read that I will definitely be playing in the Leeds first team next day against Leicester City. I do a light training session at Elland Road. It involves two five-a-side teams. Don Revie coaches one and Les Cocker the other.

At twelve o'clock I go for my first medical test. It is an electro-cardiograph test of the heart. Then on to a Leeds hospital for a blood test.

From there I go to a big house that seems to have a specialist in every room. By 2.30 p.m. I am finished with the specialists. Nobody seems the slightest bit concerned. And I couldn't be happier.

I go back to the hotel, watch the last two TV races, have an early tea — then go for a walk around Leeds on my own to get to know the place.

## NOVEMBER 6

SATURDAY! My big day. When I am to turn out for the team I have always admired.

Don Revie is to pick me up at 10.30 to take me to the hotel where Leeds have their meal before the game.

We have a cup of coffee in the lounge and he tells me I must go to see ANOTHER specialist that very morning.

Right then I begin to worry a little. We go back to the big house. I have some more tests.

We get back into Mr Revie's car. I think we are now going to the team's hotel for lunch. But I begin to recognise the streets. We are going back to my hotel. What now? I think.

We go into the lounge and sit down. Then Mr Revie says — "This is the hardest thing I have ever had to tell anyone. We cannot sign you. You will have to go back to West Brom."

In a daze I ask him — "What is wrong?"

"You have a heart murmur," he says. "I'm sorry.

# ASA HARTFORD REMEMBERS . . .

ON Wednesday, November 3rd, last season ASA HARTFORD (West Bromwich Albion and Scotland) began a nightmare experience.

It was to thrust him on to the front page of every newspaper.

For, suddenly, his £170,000 transfer to Leeds United was stopped — because he was reported to have a heart condition.

For fourteen days this little Scotsman lived on the razor edge, his career in danger, while exhaustive medical tests were carried out.

Eventually came clearance, relief — and successful comeback to the international field.

Here Asa Hartford looks back on these fourteen momentous days . . .

Do not worry. I suggest you go back to your girl friend's house in West Bromwich."

I leave Leeds in my car at 11.55 a.m. As I drive down the motorway I hear the news on the radio. They say the signing would not be completed because I have a heart abnormality,

Then I begin to worry about the effect this news may have on my fiancee — now my wife — Joy Francis. I stop at four telephone boxes off the motorway. All are out of order. I know she watches Grandstand on TV and that the news will probably be on that or "On The Ball."

I arrive at Joy's house at about 2.30. The minute I see her face I know she knows. I quickly assure her I feel perfectly O K.

At 2.45 p.m. a limousine arrives at the house and I am told to report to The Hawthorns. I see my manager, Mr Don Howe. He says that I have to see the chairman, Mr Gaunt.

Mr Gaunt reassures me — "Whatever happens," he says, "we will look after you. Even if you have to retire from the game."

I watch West Brom play. They are beaten 1-0 by Stoke City. At the end my problem is how to get out of the ground. One hour after the match there are hundreds of fans and Press men and TV people waiting to interview me.

# DAYS...

**ASA HARTFORD**

Eventually I am smuggled out a side entrance in a groundsman's van — and am booked into a secret hotel to protect me from too many questions.

My mate at West Brom, Len Cantello, comes round to the hotel. We sneak out and drive into the country, yarning about the fantastic events of the day.

Joy's mum and dad come round to the hotel in the early evening and we have dinner together. They are all very upset. Her mum is crying and so is Joy. But I am not the slightest bit worried. I try to reassure them it will turn out O K in the end.

### NOVEMBER 8

IN the morning I listen to the wireless. Once again there is plenty of news about me. Then I read all the papers. Some of the West Brom lads come round at lunchtime.

In the afternoon I go out to see a top heart specialist — Dr Paul Davison. After some tests he says that I definitely have a small hole in the upper part of my heart.

He says there are two tests he can do to show whether there will be any danger to my health from playing football. One of these tests takes quite a while.

The other is much more easily done. I do the easy, quick test.

The doctor tells me I need have no fears about playing football at top level. The hole is not large enough to cause any damage.

I go to the ground and train for 55 minutes — full out. There are TV cameras all round the training pitch. To me it's a dawdle. But afterwards the Press men and TV interviewers want to know how hard it was for me.

My manager, Don Howe, takes me into a room upstairs at our training centre. He tells the interviewers they can ask me six questions — and that is all!

### NOVEMBER 12

TODAY I learn that I am in the Scotland pool for the match against Holland in Amsterdam on December 1.

Obviously Scotland's team manager, Tommy Docherty, does not fear any weakness in my game because of the heart condition. That selection is a wonderful boost to my spirits.

### NOVEMBER 13

I AM back in the West Brom first team to play Nottingham Forest away. Coming down the tunnel I can hear the fans chanting my name. "Asa! Asa! Asa!"

The noise that hits me as I came out on to the pitch is shattering. Those fans are fantastic.

The first time I kick the ball the cheer is tremendous. I can't get it out of my head.

We lose 1-4 and everybody says I played well. I do not think so. But there is still one heart test to take.

The big one the Midlands specialist feels will put all doubts about my future beyond doubt. That is set up for the following Wednesday.

### NOVEMBER 17

I GO to a Birmingham hospital for the test. I strip and the specialist puts a thin tube into a vein in my arm. Then they start to push it through the vein to my heart.

Above me is a TV set on which I can watch the progress of the tube. It goes up my arm and twists through my chest and stops in the middle of my heart. This is a strange feeling, but there is no pain.

The tube, I am told, has stopped at the tiny hole in my heart. From examination the specialist can tell there is absolutely no danger to my health.

The hole is smaller than a pinhead. The heart is strong.

There is no danger . . .

BRYAN KING, Millwall

I'D LIKE TO PLAY FULL BACK

*Says*

**RALPH COATES**
OF SPURS

*— here (white jersey) with
Harry Burrows (Stoke City)*

THE first medal I ever won in professional football has a special place in my new house in Hertfordshire.

It deserves to. I call it my £190,000 medal.

That was the fee that took me from Burnley to Spurs just over 18 months ago and I picked up that "gong" six weeks later.

It was like going to a new world, joining Spurs from Burnley. And, saying that, I'm not knocking Burnley. They were a great club in every way.

I spent ten happy years at Turf Moor. They will always be "my" club. After Spurs matches, my first thought is — " I wonder how Burnley got on?"

113

# Manager Nicholson's High-Power "Strolls"

The darned thing is, that in those ten years with Burnley I never won anything.

They are, of course, a small town club. True, they were League Champions not so long ago. But, these days, it would be almost impossible to repeat that feat. They have to sell players to pay their way now.

Anyhow, after ten years in the game a player with ambition has to look towards one of the bigger clubs.

That medal of mine is a winner's award from last season's Anglo-Italian Cup competition. Spurs, as League Cup holders, played home and away games against Italian Cup winners Torino. We won 3-0 on aggregate.

I was pleased as punch. The other players took it as a matter of course. I found that when, after the presentation, I stood in the dressing-room admiring my medal.

"Haven't you got any of those at home?" said one of the other lads. "When I want my medals cleaned I have to hire a furniture van!"

That was the big difference between Burnley and Spurs. The Spurs lads expect to win. They have a touch of arrogance.

I'd heard a lot about the Spurs' fans in the weeks before playing my first match for the club. How they'd given big-money signings like Martin Chivers, Martin Peters and Terry Venables a tough time at first.

I was apprehensive. And glad I was playing my first game at Wolverhampton. But, when it came to the crunch, the Spurs' crowd couldn't have treated me better. I like playing at home now.

The £190,000 fee never really worried me. For a start, Bill Nicholson put me at ease soon as I signed.

"Don't worry about the transfer fee," he said. "If the fans are looking for someone to lynch they'll be after me first!"

On that first morning we had a training walk. "Just a stroll round Cheshunt," said Phil Beal.

As Mr Nicholson was to lead the way, I reckoned it would be just that. A loosener in preparation for the harder work. How wrong can you be?

Bill Nicholson walks faster than many players run! I had to run to keep up. And we walked miles!

After about an hour I asked one of the lads how much farther. His answer was—"Just round the corner." Some corner. The "stroll" lasted another five miles! I was absolutely exhausted at the end—but Bill Nicholson was still striding away at the front.

A lot of things continued to surprise me in my early days at White Hart Lane. The form and fitness of Alan Gilzean, for example.

Only by playing alongside "Gillie" is it possible to realise how good he is. He's so skilful in the air I reckon he could head goals with a haggis in place of a ball. He can place a header exactly where he wants to. He's mighty accurate with his feet, too.

It always used to shock me in training when, after a flat-out sprint, I'd turn to find Gillie right at my shoulder. I only hope I'm half as good and fit when I've reached the same age.

It was European football that really made me want

to join a club like Spurs. At Burnley I'd watch the European matches on the television, and desperately want to be part of it.

In my first season with Spurs we played in the U.E.F.A. Cup. This was what top football is all about. Meeting teams in Iceland, Italy, France and Rumania.

While winning some England caps with Burnley I thought my international prospects would be better with a bigger club. I often thought about buying Sir Alf Ramsey a map showing the way to the town. For sake of all the fine players there.

Yet England gave me my biggest disappointment. It was awful missing the 1970 World Cup after being included in the initial party. I was one of the six unlucky ones who dropped out before the show got started.

I was so downcast I took myself off to Spain for a month's holiday. At the time I felt I never wanted to see another football.

It was a game of beach football that jerked me out of this mood. I was asked to play for a local side, Los Magnificos, against a team of German holiday-makers and Spanish waiters.

**ALAN GILZEAN**

It was just an enjoyable kick-around. Everything relaxed and free and easy. I enjoyed it so much I returned from holiday eager to get back in the swing with Burnley.

I was even more eager to get going the next year—after joining Spurs. But that was only after overcoming all my doubts about the move.

For, the day after signing the transfer forms, I was all set to call it all off! The thought of moving to the stir of London started to worry me.

I had pretty well made up my mind to ring Spurs first thing in the morning and tell them—when the phone rang.

It was a reporter wanting to know all about the transfer. The news was out. There was no going back. Talking to people afterwards dispelled all my fears. I became sure I'd done the right thing. Now I know . . .

I don't mind where I play in the team. But, I admit, I prefer midfield. So last season's unlucky injury to Alan Mullery actually helped me settle in.

Obviously we'd have preferred to have Alan in the team. But, from a personal viewpoint, being able to play in midfield was a tremendous help.

At Burnley I had a free hand. I could go anywhere in search of the ball. That's the role which suits me best—but it's still not my favourite position.

GIVEN THE CHANCE, I'D LIKE TO PLAY AT FULL-BACK!

That's the position I always pick in training games if we ever switch about. I first tried it at Burnley and always found that I could "read" the winger. As I'm quite quick, very few forwards got past me in practice.

I used to break Steve Kindon's heart in training. He never got by me. He has even called me the best full-back he has ever faced!

Perhaps I'll switch to full-back when I'm past it in midfield. I reckon I could play there till I'm 45!

114

# DESPERATE MOMENTS

## HOW THE SPLIT-SECOND CAMERA CAN GIVE A PICTURE THAT SOMETHING EXTRA . . .

Kick on the chin — looking to be on the cards for PETER OSGOOD, Chelsea, as JOHN ROBERTS, Arsenal, flies between him and team-mate FRANK McLINTOCK.

Stranglehold — apparently exerted by WILLIE JOHNSTON, Rangers, on JIM BROGAN, Celtic.

DAVE WEBB, Chelsea — seemingly about to land a haymaker on FRANK WIGNALL, Derby County, now Mansfield Town.

# RIGHT DRESS....

**ABERDEEN**

Left to right—Back row—Mr R. Donald (Chairman), Drew Jarvie, Jim Hermiston, Arthur Graham, George Murray, Bertie Miller, Dave Robb, Andy Geoghan, Ian Taylor, Henning Boel, Tommy McMillan (now Falkirk), Barrie Mitchell. Front Row—Mr J. Bonthrone (Manager), R. Coutts (Physiotherapist), George Buchan, Alec Willoughby, Jim Forrest, Steve Murray, Tom Wilson, Joe Harper, Willie Young.

**QUEEN'S PARK**     Left to right—Back row—G. Miller, J. Logan, J. McLean.
Middle row—J. Strang, J. Eadie, J. Taylor, R. McNaught, R. Hart, P.F. Jones.
Front row—A. Richmond , L.H. Skene, T.F. Campbell, A. Dalziel, D. Wilson, jnr., E.C. Crawford, A.J. Nisbet.

116

SPECIAL occasion—so clubs fit players out with special off-field "uniforms."

It's the done thing nowadays . . .

Here (left) is the ABERDEEN party pictured before setting off for their summer-time tour in U.S.A. and Canada.

A smart lot they look in their dark blazers and trousers, white shirts and club ties.

Below—LEEDS UNITED parade their F.A. Cup Final suits—in which they went to Wembley and pulled off victory.

And how about the company bottom left?

For the famous QUEEN'S PARK amateur side around the early 1900's it was all strictly "go-as-you-please" for players as far as off-field dress was concerned.

Straw "boaters" can be seen in the party—but trilby hats and bowlers were all the go when picture No. 4 was taken.

In the fashion are JACK HARKNESS (Hearts) and the late ALEC JACKSON (Chelsea) when they were Scotland team members of the 1920's. Notice their spats, too!

Left—Jack Harkness
—and Alec Jackson.

### LEEDS UNITED

Left to right—Billy Bremner (Captain), Johnny Giles, Mick Bates, Paul Reaney, Peter Lorimer, Terry Yorath, Eddie Gray, Mick Jones, Paul Madeley (half hidden), Joe Jordan, Gary Sprake, Norman Hunter, Allan Clarke.

# MY KIND OF CARTOONS

Chosen by
**PAT JENNINGS, Spurs**

"They'll no' throw the book at him—he can't read!"

"I'm wearin' my teeth next half . . . he's just bitten me!"

"Get out of town!"

"A long lofted kick from his own half, its bounce has beaten the back . . . it's going . . .!"

"They won by nine lucky goals!!"

# IT ALL MADE NEWS LAST SEASON

1—He was introduced to the crowd as the club's new record buy—but played for another club the following Saturday. Who was player and which clubs involved?

2—**Which club in Britain were first to know they would be relegated?**

3—A start-of-season free transfer man ended up playing for both Scottish League champions and runners-up. Who was he?

4—**He broke his club's scoring record — then finished the season in hospital. Do you know his name?**

5—For the first time, two British teams met in the final of a European competition. Which teams? Which tournament?

6—**Four clubs fought out the First Division championship until the last kick. Which clubs, and in what order did they finish?**

7—A non-league side hit the headlines on February 6. Which club? What occasion?

8—**He scored his first hat-trick for his new club in Scottish Cup Final. Who?**

9—Northampton Town established an unenviable record. What was it?

10—**When the season started the young fellow pictured here was fourth in the queue for his team's left-back position. When it ended he was first choice and a full international. His name?**

11—They won 2-0 away in a European competition—then were beaten 4-0 at home in the second leg. Which club? Which competition?

12—**Stoke City figured in an unusual double—two out-field players kept goal against them in important cup-ties. The players and matches?**

13—When the season opened, two clubs were banned from playing any games on their home grounds. Who were they?

14—**Name the eight clubs who won promotion in England.**

15—He created a Scottish transfer record in leaving his former club, but wore the same colours in the English First Division. His name?

16—**Who were " Footballers of the Year " in England and Scotland?**

17—They won their first major trophy after 108 years of trying. Which club? What trophy?

18—**Partick Thistle won the Scottish League Cup. Whom did they beat and what was the score?**

19—Which club fielded in their final league game the same team that took the field in the first match of the season?

20—**A famous internationalist was loaned from one club to another, then returned to play in a vital cup-tie. The player, clubs involved, and what was the occasion?**

21—Rangers made the European Cup-winners' final by defeating French, Italian and German opposition. Which teams?

Answers on page 122

# BOBBY CHARLTON

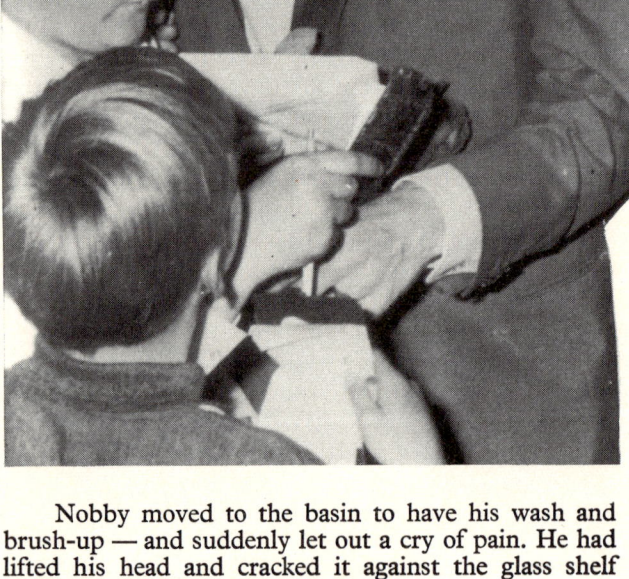

**N**OBODY will ever get me to start a cycle race again.

I'll see to that!

For I'm the fellow who RUINED the take-off for the great Tour of Ireland event.

On the same day as the Tour was to get going, Manchester United were playing Waterford in the European Cup.

I always rise early in the morning. On match days most others stay in bed until about 10.30 a.m. or so.

An official from the tour organisers came into our hotel and asked me if I would start the race. Yes, I told him — as long as I could then get straight back into the hotel.

Well, the race started just across the street. There were thousands of football fans gathered outside our hotel. And they all seemed to want my autograph.

They pressed forward, hemming me in. There was no chance of my getting to the starting line for the race, so I appealed for silence and yelled out—" As soon as I have got the cyclists away I'll sign all your books.''

I dropped a flag to start the race — and suddenly the street was jammed with people. They all rushed at me. It was like being in the middle of a rugby scrum. The cyclists could not get away. There was no way through!

So, while I signed for the fans, the police made a narrow passageway through the crowd and the cyclists pedalled off one at a time. I can imagine what they were calling me.

That is an occasion I can look back on and laugh about. My pal Nobby Stiles has a million like it.

Let me tell you Nobby is the most accident-prone player you'll ever meet OFF the field. He is practically a walking disaster area.

I always shared a room with him on tour with England. We were in Yugoslavia one trip and had asked for an 8.30 a.m. call to be in time for a plane.

The call didn't come until 9.00. We were in a hurry then. I got myself washed and shaved in the room hand-basin.

Nobby moved to the basin to have his wash and brush-up — and suddenly let out a cry of pain. He had lifted his head and cracked it against the glass shelf above the basin, inflicting a cut.

Then he went over to open the curtains. He pulled the cord. Both drapes fell to the floor!

Minutes later we were dressed and ready to go. Nobby made to switch the radio off. It was attached to the wall. As he turned the switch the set fell off that wall!

It was all so typical . . .

Nor will any of us in the England team forget the day Nobby finished a meal, stood up, walked away from the table — and pulled off the tablecloth. It had somehow caught in his shoe!

# WHAT A BASHING I TOOK AT THE BIKE RACE

I kept it out of Nobby's hands throughout the entire trip. But, when we were leaving Australia, I slipped up . . . for about 30 seconds.

I had two small carrier bags. One contained a couple of bottles of wine. In the other was the camera. I asked Nobby to hold them for a second while I bought a newspaper.

He decided to save me the trouble of carrying two bags and tried to put the camera in with the bottles. You've guessed. He dropped the bag. The bottles smashed. The camera was badly damaged.

Trips abroad can have their funny moments. It's not all sweat and nervous tension. There is certainly no shortage of England players to keep the laughs going.

Alan Ball, for instance, has one prank that can cause surprise first thing in the morning.

In many hotels abroad there is a menu card on the wall outside each bedroom. If anyone wants breakfast served there — and most of the England team do — it's simply a question of marking what's wanted on the card.

"Ballie" has a habit of sneaking into the corridor late at night and filling in other players' menu cards.

One morning a trolley was wheeled into my room laden with the biggest breakfast anybody ever faced.

Grilled bloaters, porridge, biscuits, hot chocolate, scrambled eggs, tea and toast, grapefruit, rolls and jam.

That was my first experience of "Ballie" on the ball. But it has happened since . . .

You can imagine food plays a big part in players' lives abroad. Sometimes the biggest problems come AFTER the game when we are invited out by people in the countries we visit.

You see, everybody seems to want to show greater hospitality than the other. And first rule always seems to be to serve up the best meal they can manage. That usually means the BIGGEST.

In Italy I was guest of a football fan in a local restaurant. The meal I ate had eight courses — pate, salami, pasta, soup, steak, Italian cheeses, coffee ice-cream, fruit and coffee. On top of that, four different wines were served.

Another memory of Nobby starts with the crash of breaking dishes in the upstairs lounge at London Airport.

Our flight had been delayed and the airport people told Sir Alf Ramsey we could all go upstairs and wait in the V.I.P. lounge.

Nobby was last in line as we all walked up a long corridor. We passed a trolley laden with food and dishes. Suddenly there was a crash.

Without looking round, one or two of us said, "That'll be Nobby."

Sure enough — it was. He had walked straight into the trolley!

You'll have got the message on Nobby. But one last little yarn of a moment that cost me dearly.

I usually carry around a movie camera when travelling. On this particular trip — to Australia via U.S.A., Honolulu and New Zealand — I took an expensive still camera loaned by a Manchester neighbour.

# How I Found My "Long-Lost" Uncle

In all, that spread took three and a half hours to eat!

Sometimes Sir Alf Ramsey tells the cook of our hotel that he should ask the team what they want for dinner. When that happens, we usually choose one player who decides what the order will be.

Given the chance one day, I chose a typical English dish — roast beef, sprouts, roast potatoes and Yorkshire pudding. The chef was so pleased with the challenge. He stuck his chest out and promised us an English dinner to remember.

But when it arrived the Yorkshire pudding was like a wet lump of dough. It kept the jaws going like with chewing-gum. I was banned from picking the meal again.

There is one aspect of travelling I have never been able to solve. That is sleeping on aeroplanes.

I have travelled hundreds of thousands of miles by air. Never once have I been able to stay asleep while in flight.

Bobby Charlton has become, in the football world, a famous name. I realise that.

When I go abroad, I am often surprised and delighted to meet fans who have sent me telegrams and people who write me letters.

There is one who stands out. His name is Jose. He lives in Mexico and has been writing me since 1957. Whenever I am in Mexico I take time out to see him.

Then again, back home in Manchester, are two fans whom I never met until this year. Yet for 10 years they had been sending me telegrams wishing me luck before big games with United and England.

The signatures were — Biddy and Eve.

So, some time ago, I decided to get their address and visit them. They were two gentle lady spinsters. I had tea with them. I think they were in business.

I have always been most grateful to fans who have followed my career with so much enthusiasm. I have never employed anybody in the nature of a secretary to deal with fan mail. I always wanted to give it my personal attention.

Now let me tell you about the time I went on tour to Australia — hoping to meet a " long lost " uncle.

From my very young days back in Ashington I remembered my Uncle Matthew because he used to send biscuits from Australia. They did not taste any different from British biscuits, but they had Australia stamped on them and I used to take them to school. They were a novelty and all the other kids wanted to eat them.

They came to us regularly, and, naturally, Uncle Matthew was in my mind when we landed in Australia. I had never met him. I didn't know where he lived.

Anyway, it seemed from the start every person in Australia called Charlton was determined to find out if I was a relation. On my first day the phone in my hotel room never stopped ringing.

Conversations would go something like this — " Hello, Bobby. My name is Ethel. I have relations in Brighton, England. I wonder if you are related to me Could I come and meet you?"

This went on and on. Naturally, I wanted some peace. But I managed to keep everybody happy.

Then we reached Perth at the end of our tour.

Outside our hotel a man stepped in front of me.

Pointing at a figure a few yards away, he said, " You know who that is, don't you?"

" Sorry, I don't," I replied.

" Oh, yes, you do," said the stranger. " It's your Uncle Matthew!"

And there he was — the very man I'd wanted so long to meet.

We went off to talk about biscuits and the family.

---

## IT ALL MADE NEWS LAST SEASON

1—Ian Moore. Derby County thought his transfer from Nottingham Forest was sewn up — until Manchester United stepped in.

2—Watford, relegated from Second Division to Third. Their fate was sealed early April.

3—Gordon Marshall (Celtic and Aberdeen). Now with Arbroath.

4—Francis Lee of Manchester City with 33 goals. He went into hospital suffering from physical and mental exhaustion.

5—Spurs and Wolves met in the U.E.F.A. Cup Final. Spurs won 3-2 (agg).

6—Derby County, Leeds United, Liverpool and Manchester City— who finished in that order. Derby were on 58 points, the others on 57.

7—Hereford United, when they knocked out Newcastle United in the F.A. Cup third round replay.

8—Dixie Deans (Celtic).

9—Seven years ago they were in Division One. Last season they had to apply for re-election to the Fourth.

10—Willie Donachie of Manchester City and Scotland. He queue-jumped David Connor (now Preston), Arthur Mann and injured Glyn Pardoe.

11—Leeds United, in the U.E.F.A. Cup-tie against Lierse of Belgium.

12—In the F.A. Cup semi-final, Arsenal 'keeper Bob Wilson tore a ligament. John Radford went in goal. In the League Cup semi, Bobby Ferguson of West Ham received a head injury. Bobby Moore took over as 'keeper.

13—Leeds United (four home games) and Manchester United (two). Elland Road and Old Trafford were closed following crowd trouble.

14—Norwich City and Birmingham from Second to First; Aston Villa and Brighton from Third to Second; Grimsby, Southend, Brentford and Scunthorpe from Fourth to Third.

15—Martin Buchan (Aberdeen to Manchester United.)

16—England — Gordon Banks (Stoke City). Scotland—Dave Smith (Rangers).

17—Stoke City. They beat Chelsea 2-1 in the League Cup Final.

18—Celtic (4-1).

19—Millwall. The team was—King; Brown, Cripps; Dorney, Kitchener, Burnett; Possee, Bolland, Bridges, Dunphy and Allder.

20—Alan Mullery. Loaned from Spurs to Fulham, he returned to White Hart Lane the day before he turned out for them in the U.E.F.A. Cup semi-final against A.C. Milan.

21—Rennes (France), Torino (Italy), Bayern Munich (Germany).

**Answers to Quiz on page 119**

# THE CROCK WHO TALKED HIS TEAM TO VICTORY

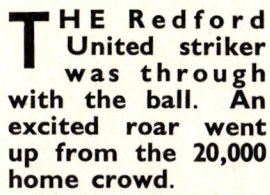

**T**HE Redford United striker was through with the ball. An excited roar went up from the 20,000 home crowd.

The goalkeeper came plunging out. The striker shot. A groan went up from every home fan as the ball soared high over the bar.

One man in the crowd had not joined in the shouting — or the groans. He stood quietly behind a barrier, unnoticed by those around him.

He was about thirty, stocky and muscular. He wore an old sports jacket. His hair was cropped short under a tweed cap. He seemed unaffected by the excitement of the crowd, but his eyes were shrewd and watchful, missing nothing that happened on the field.

The visiting team, Framley Rovers, moved into attack.

The United defence scrambled back. Framley's winger danced the ball towards the corner flag and lifted it across. In the goalmouth, two United defenders hesitated, each leaving the ball to the other. The Framley striker burst between them. He slammed a shot into the net before the 'keeper had moved.

A howl of disappointment from the home crowd mingled with the cheers of the Framley fans. The man in the tweed cap remained expressionless—showing no sign of emotion.

Framley came back again, piling on the pressure, creating panic in the home defence. United's left-back slashed at the ball to clear. It spun away into the net, out of the 'keeper's reach.

The third goal came soon after half-time. With three in the bag, Framley began to ease up. But the United still found it impossible to get through.

The Framley right-back broke up an attack by banging the ball into touch. It bounced near the spot where the man in the tweed cap was standing. He leaned over the barrier and grabbed the ball.

Dave Paterson, the United No. 4, ran across to take the throw-in, but the man in the tweed cap still held on to the ball.

Dave Paterson crossed the track to claim it.

"Switch your striker out to the left," said the man in the tweed cap. "Tell him to keep pressing down that wing."

"If you think you can do better, get out there and try, mate!" grunted Dave. Hardly glancing at the man, he snatched the ball.

Bob Harper, the grey-haired manager of United, leaned from his dug-out to see what was causing delay. He stared at the man in the tweed cap.

"Hey, I think that's Joe Langley in the crowd!" he exclaimed to his trainer. "A former World Cup player on the terraces! I'm ashamed a player like Langley should see all this."

Dave Paterson took the throw. He hurled the ball into the middle. The United striker took two paces with it and was robbed by the Framley centre-half.

The ball was back in the United half. A desperate sliding tackle by a United defender brought down the Framley inside-left. The referee's whistle shrilled. The Framley striker made no mistake from the spot.

The Framley supporters were beginning to chant, "Easy, easy!" There was no response from the home crowd. Many were already drifting away.

# MAGIC IN THE No. 11 JERSEY

United managed to hold the score at that until the final whistle, but left the field a well-beaten team. Manager Bob Harper hurried from the dug-out to where the man in the tweed cap was standing.

"Joe Langley!" said Bob Harper. "What are you doing here? If you'd told me you were coming I'd have got you a seat in the stand."

"The terracing suits me," said Langley. "I had to come to Redford to see a specialist about my leg. I dropped in to see the game afterwards."

"That injury was bad luck," said Harper. "I was sorry to hear your club has given you a free transfer. You should have some football years left yet. What did the specialist say?"

"The same as my club," grunted Langley. "I'm finished with the game."

The television commentator left his box, carrying a hand microphone. He was followed by a man with a portable camera.

"I'll try to get a word with Bob Harper about the game," he said into the microphone. "Hello, if that's not Joe Langley! The opinion of a former star should be interesting!" He thrust the microphone forward. "What's your verdict on United, Joe?"

"They're the most promising team I've seen for a long time," answered Joe.

"What? You must be joking! They lost 4-0!"

"I'm serious. They have the potential to be a great side."

"Well, after that, what is there for me to add?" said the commentator, turning away. "I imagine the viewers are as surprised as I am!"

Joe Langley started to walk away. Harper grabbed his arm.

"You meant that, Joe!" exclaimed Harper. "Listen, I've got a great idea! Join us as a coach. You could lick them into shape, I'm sure of it."

"I'd like to try," answered Joe. "But I don't want to be a coach. Give me a go in the team!"

Harper stared at him. "In the team? But you're crocked!"

"I'm not so fast as I was, but I can still get around. What your side needs is somebody out there on the field to pull them together. That's what I can do for you."

"Yes, you always had a good football brain, Joe. And I never saw you flap. It's experience like yours our lads are short of."

"I'm not finished yet, whatever my old club and the doctors say."

Harper stuck out his hand. "You're in, Joe!"

* * * *

The United players stood in a group on their training pitch. Joe Langley trotted towards them, wearing a tracksuit. He had a ball at his feet.

"Is that the best he can do?" muttered Dave Paterson. "A slow old man is no use to us!"

"Come and get it off me," Joe called.

Dave winked at the others. He raced across to Joe and went sliding in. Joe did not increase speed, but his feet did a sudden shuffle. Then he moved on, still in possession. Dave skated by — and ended up on his back.

Joe stopped and watched Dave getting to his feet.

"You signalled that from the moment you started running," he said.

"All right," grunted Dave. "You've made your point! You can still play—in slow motion!"

"That's about it," said Joe, unruffled. "I'll supply the brains and you fellows add the legs!"

Bob Harper approached and beckoned. Joe moved aside to join the manager.

"Somebody's got to be dropped to make room for you in our next game against Brampton City, Joe," said Harper.

"Tony Dawson, the No. 11, is the youngest and rawest of the lot," came back Joe. "It won't hurt him to sit it out as substitute. I'll go in as 11. I can potter on the wing and keep an eye on things from there."

"All right, Joe," agreed Harper. "And I'm naming you as captain."

The inclusion of Joe Langley in the team was big news. Reporters were waiting when United arrived at the Brampton City stadium.

A roar greeted the United as Joe led them out. A large party of fans had travelled to Brampton to see what the newspapers were calling "The Crock's Comeback."

Joe won the toss. Brampton kicked off with a slight breeze behind them. Dave Paterson ran in for a tackle and was beaten. The ball lifted into the United goal area. The two United backs moved in together.

A voice bellowed across the pitch. Joe had come trotting back. "Yours, Bill!" he roared.

Bill Simmonds, the United left-back, went for the ball. Frank Martin, the other defender, fell back to cover the goal. "Bring it up!" shouted Joe.

Bill Simmonds brought the ball along. He pushed it along the wing to Joe. Without moving from where he was standing, Joe hooked the ball across into the middle. "Go right, Terry!" he ordered.

Terry Jackson pounced on the ball. Swiftly it was swung across to the right. The defence shifted to cover him. "Over here, Peter!" roared Joe.

He pointed to a gap that had opened up in the defence. Peter Willis, United's No. 8, came sprinting through. Terry Jackson swerved away from a defender and put the ball across. Peter ran on to it and hit it first time. The shot hurtled just wide of the post.

Peter came across to Joe. He was angry with himself. "Sorry, Joe," he said. "You worked that out for us and then I went and muffed it."

"Don't be daft!" said Joe. "That was a great try!"

Peter grinned and strode away.

Brampton came back strongly. Dave Paterson went at the man in possession in his usual bull-at-a-gate style. The Brampton man checked. Dave slithered past, and the Brampton forward strode on.

The ball swung into the middle. The Brampton striker hit it. The ball shot towards the United goal, wide of the goalkeeper. Joe Langley was standing on the line. He headed away, and Bill Simmonds booted the ball into touch.

"Thanks, Joe," gasped the goal-

# THE VOICE OF INSPIRATION

keeper. "They caught me out of position there."

"You'll be all right if you come out quicker to cut off the crosses, lad," said Joe.

He trotted away and spoke to Dave Paterson.

"Go for the ball, not the man," he said. "It's no fun being on the free-transfer list! I know!"

"A free transfer?" exclaimed Dave. His face went red. "Me? I'll show you!"

He hitched up his sleeves and moved away for the throw-in. Terry Jackson was within earshot.

"You were a bit rough with Dave," he said. "I haven't heard you speak to anybody else like that, Joe."

"Some fellows need a bit of quiet encouragement, others want a prod," answered Joe. "Dave's the sort that likes a fight. He'll play a great game now, just to prove me wrong!"

The ball came in from the Brampton throw. Dave Paterson jabbed out a foot and hooked it away from the player it was intended for. Beating a man, Dave strode away fast. He swerved left, cut in as the back loomed up and chopped a pass across to Terry Jackson.

Terry hit a screamer. The goalkeeper just got his fingers to it and tipped over the bar. Joe trotted away to take the corner.

He put an in-swinger down in the goalmouth. Terry climbed into the air and headed the ball back. Dave Paterson ran on and slammed a shot through a gap in the ruck of players. The ball was bobbing in the back of the net before the goalkeeper realised what was happening.

"How was that?" Dave asked Joe, defiantly.

"You're improving!" said Joe.

Brampton tried to hit back, but United held them. Despite his slowness, Joe Langley seemed to bob up everywhere. He talked all the time, giving instructions and encouragement, persuading and driving.

At half-time the United were still hanging on to their one-goal lead.

"We're doing all right!" said Dave, in the dressing-room.

"One goal isn't enough against a team like Brampton City," said Joe. "We need more."

But it was Brampton who scored first. They attacked down the middle. A gust of wind caught the ball and made it swerve away from a United defender. The Brampton striker ran on to it and banged it into the net.

Joe was after his team immediately. "Keep at 'em, lads!" he shouted. "Don't give them time to draw breath! They're kicking into the wind. They'll tire before we do. That's what we want."

United obeyed. They pushed the ball about beautifully. Soon the Brampton defence were under constant pressure.

Joe trotted up and down, not often in action but watching every move. He talked his team through the game, keeping up his flow of advice and encouragement.

"I'm fed up with the sound of your voice!" the Brampton striker said to him.

"You'll be even more fed up when you hear me cheering our winning goal!" Joe grinned.

He moved out to the wing. The ball came out to him, hit low by Dave Paterson. Joe made ground, went round the back at what seemed a walking pace and pushed the ball into the middle. Terry Jackson was brought down as he tried to take it.

Joe trotted over to take the free kick. He gave a nod, and the United players moved into positions he had rehearsed.

A wall of Brampton players formed up. Terry Jackson pushed in alongside. Joe took a couple of paces. He seemed to be shaping to blast the ball at Terry. At the last second he changed pace and chipped the ball away. The wind caught it and lofted it left.

Peter Willis had drifted that way and was standing unmarked. He chested the ball down and was past the wall of defenders. The goalkeeper dived too late as the ball lashed into the net.

"Let's have another, lads!" said Joe.

United were full of confidence now. They forged ahead, keeping Brampton at full stretch.

"Brampton are tiring!" exclaimed the United trainer. "I've never seen our lads play like this."

"Joe's made a team out of a bunch of talented individuals," said Bob Harper.

United kept up the pressure. A long clearance by Bill Simmonds was carried by the wind into the Brampton half. Joe bobbed up in the middle and brought the ball along. A defender pounded across. Joe side-footed the ball. Terry Jackson strode past, collected the pass, and hit a rising shot from thirty yards into the top corner of the net.

With time running out, United came back again. Dave Paterson collected a pass from Joe and pushed it through to Terry. The United striker broke away. A defender hurled himself across in a desperate tackle. Down went Terry. The referee's whistle shrilled. A roar went up from the United fans.

"Penalty!"

"Come on, Dave," said Joe. "You're our penalty man."

Dave looked at the other players, then shook his head.

"No, this one's yours, Joe!"

"That's right, Joe," grinned Terry Jackson. "You've been doing the talking for nearly ninety minutes. Now it's our turn! Bang it in!"

Joe put the ball on the penalty spot. He went back a couple of paces, trotted forward and connected. It seemed almost casual, but the 'keeper was still diving the wrong way as the ball landed in the net.

The roar of the crowd almost drowned the sound of the referee's whistle as he blew for full-time. The United players slapped Joe on the back.

"4-1!" grinned Dave Paterson. He held out his hand. "Thanks for the football lesson, skipper!"

"We're only just starting," said Joe. "I've got ten years' experience to pass on to you fellows!"

"Will your legs hold out?" asked Terry.

"I'm not worrying about my legs," said Joe. "If I do have to pack up I'll be the first footballer dropped because his voice gave out."

Printed and Published by D. C. Thomson & Co., Ltd., 12 Fetter Lane, Fleet Street, London, E.C.4.
© D. C. Thomson & Co., Ltd., 1972.